PICASSO, MOZART, and YOU

PICASSO, MOZART, and YOU

A GUIDE TO CREATIVITY

George Domino, Ph.D.

Published in the United States of America by:

Imago Press
3710 East Edison
Tucson AZ 85716
www.imagobooks.com

Library of Congress Cataloging-in-Publication Data

Domino, George, 1938-
Picasso, Mozart, and you : unleashing your creative self / George Domino.
p. cm.
Includes bibliographical references.
ISBN-13: 978-1-935437-01-7 (pbk. : alk. paper)
ISBN-10: 1-935437-01-1 (pbk. : alk. paper)
1. Creative ability. I. Title.
BF408.D62 2009
153.3'5--dc22

2009004619

Book and Cover Design by Leila Joiner
Cover art "Abstract Composition" © FotoliaI (Infinite Collection)

ISBN 978-1-935437-01-7
ISBN 1-935437-01-1

Printed in the United States of America on Acid-Free Paper

Table of Contents

Chapter 1

The Nature and Nurture of Creativity

What Is Creativity?

Creativity is fun and exciting; it can be challenging and personally fulfilling. Someone once asked Willie Sutton, the infamous bank robber, why he robbed so many banks. He replied, "Because that's where the money is." So why be creative? Because that's where the fun is.

Albert Szent-Gyorgyi, the Nobel prize-winning physician, said, "Discovery consists of looking at the same thing as everyone else and thinking something different."

But what is creativity? Are we talking about something mysterious that applies only to a few people like Einstein and DaVinci, or are we talking about a set of abilities and habits that applies to all of us? Many individuals who are considered highly creative have written about their own creative processes, often suggesting that creativity is a mysterious process with a life of its own. For example, both Beethoven and Mozart heard symphonies in their heads and said they had only to write down the notes. Mozart, in fact, described how these musical thoughts would crowd into his mind, and he had nothing to do with them. He simply kept in his head those that pleased him, hummed them, and they developed into a masterpiece of their own accord! Both Rimbaud and William Blake wrote that their own poetry came to them "unbidden" and almost despite themselves, and all they did was write the lines down. That's one view of creativity, and it's highly doubtful that there's any substance to it. After all, unless you have had training as a musician or a wordsmith, or have the natural talents that allow you to play "by ear," you can sit all day long waiting for creative ideas, and I guarantee you they will not come. You're not going to get tomatoes if you haven't planted tomatoes.

A different point of view, espoused in this book, is that creativity represents particular ways of thinking intertwined with one's approach to life and one's personality. As with any skill, creativity can be understood, learned, and made part of one's life, with differences between individuals as to how well they can achieve this. Obviously, not everyone can be a Michelangelo or a Picasso, no matter how much one practices, just as not every golfer can be a Ben Hogan or a Tiger Woods. But nearly everyone, with very few exceptions, can be creative.

In this first chapter, we will take a brief look at the nature of creativity and discuss a number of aspects that, hopefully, will give you a better sense of what creativity is all about. These ideas are fairly easy to understand and not at all technical, even though some are based on rather technical professional literature. In Chapter 2, we will look at the basic building blocks of creativity. We will discuss such aspects as curiosity, the passion that underlies much of creative effort, the notion of imagination as a habit, the analogical and metaphorical thinking that are required (and I'll explain these big words…), and other related topics. We will continue in Chapter 3 to look at general ways to develop and enhance creativity. There is nothing magical here—we will look at a number of techniques that have been studied, such as the use of dreams, and ways in which a person can get disparate ideas to come together in a creative solution. Finally, in Chapter 4, "The Road to Creativity," we will look at very specific ways in which one can get started on that trip. Some of the ways may already be familiar to you, such as brainstorming, the use of checklists, and the use of humor, but hopefully there will be much that is new and useful. This book contains lots of fun exercises that you can try out, as well as a number of anecdotes that may provide inspiration and a role model, such as the following:

Garrett Morgan was born in Kentucky in 1877, the son of former slaves. His formal education went only as far as elementary school, but he became a well-known inventor and businessman. He invented what was called, in 1914, a safety hood and smoke protector—i.e., a gas mask. Two years later, Morgan and other volunteers used the gas mask to rescue thirty-two men who were trapped beneath Lake Erie in an underground explosion. News accounts created a large demand for his masks, especially on the part of fire departments.

In 1907 he opened a sewing machine sales and repair shop, as well as a tailor shop that employed thirty-two workers. All the clothes produced there were sewn with equipment made by Morgan. He also invented a stitching attachment for manually operated sewing machines, and a number of other products. In 1920 he established a daily newspaper in the city of Cleveland, and by 1923 he had invented a manually operated traffic signal or, more formally, a "hand-cranked semaphore traffic management device"! This was used widely in both the United States and Canada for many years.

CREATIVITY FROM THE PERSPECTIVE OF PSYCHOLOGY

What do you think creativity is? Are you creative? Do you know someone who is creative? Would you consider Pablo Picasso or Elton John creative? In trying to answer these questions, what criteria or standards did you use? Perhaps, in your mind, someone is creative if they can play a musical instrument or paint or write poetry or engage in some artistic endeavor. Or perhaps your criteria might include a sense of humor, the ability to make puns, or to see the rational incongruity of the everyday world.

All of these are fine examples and, indeed, have been considered part of creativity by those who study creativity and by those who practice it. Paul Torrance, a psychologist who has studied creativity in great depth, defined creativity as a process that involves five steps:

1. Sensing difficulties, problems, gaps in information, missing elements, something not quite right. In other words, the ability to identify a problem that needs to be solved, a challenge that needs to be met.
2. Making guesses and formulating hypotheses about these deficiencies.
3. Evaluating and testing these guesses and hypotheses.
4. Possibly revising and retesting them.
5. Communicating the results.

It might surprise you to learn that Torrance has worked primarily with children, and his definition is grounded in his observations of children, though his description sounds more like what a scientist does in the laboratory. Notice that Torrance seems to emphasize the process of creativity rather than the creative person, and that process seems to be an "intellectual" one.

Another psychologist who has written extensively about creativity and, in fact, considers creativity a type of intelligence is Howard Gardner, a Harvard professor. Gardner considers a person creative if that person (1) regularly solves problems, (2) in a particular domain, (3) in a novel manner, (4) which sooner or later becomes accepted by a particular culture. Notice that the first component addresses the notion that creativity is habitual, is exercised regularly, and is not a one-shot phenomenon. The second component is the notion that creativity takes place in a specific domain, that the creative person is typically creative in a particular set of endeavors, like painting, engineering, poetry, or designing industrial containers. The third component is that of novelty; creativity involves doing something in a novel or unusual way. The last component is that creative efforts occur in a cultural context and, sooner or later, are inescapably judged in that context. This is not to say that creativity is recognized instantly—indeed, in many instances the opposite seems to occur. But, eventually, whether ten years later or a thousand years later, creative contributions are recognized as such. Although most of what Gardner says about creativity focuses on his notion that creativity is a particular type of intelligence, his definition focuses on the creative person rather than the process of creativity.

"Big C" and "little c"

One interesting point made by a number of psychologists, including Gardner, is that there are two types of creativity. There is "Big C" creativity, exhibited in the works of Einstein, Mozart, and Picasso. Then there is "little c" creativity, seen in everyday life—the person who creates a new recipe, or a more efficient way of doing a routine job, or one who grows bonsai trees in aesthetically pleasing shapes.

> When we hear the name, Abraham Lincoln, many images come to mind: a pivotal President, the Great Emancipator, a country lawyer, a victim of an assassin's bullet, but probably not inventor. Did you know that Abraham Lincoln is the only U.S. President to have a patent in his name? He was actually granted a patent for a flotation system to free boats that had run aground in rivers and lake areas. Lincoln's father was a mechanic, and Abraham, when not busy with his law practice, dabbled in machinery and mechanical contraptions. (Edwards, 2006)

CONVERGENT AND DIVERGENT THINKING

In this book I am going to try and avoid jargon and the technical terms that are the hallmark of any field. Some, however, we will need to face, such as convergent thinking and divergent thinking. When we try to solve a problem, most of the thinking we do is of one of two varieties. Typically, we try to solve a problem because we believe the problem has one correct answer, so our thinking tries to converge on that one right answer, and psychologists call this convergent thinking. Thus, if you try to think of the name of the 16th president of the United States, or what 9 x 26 equals, there is only one correct answer for each of these problems. But in real life we often meet problems that may have multiple solutions. The question of what to prepare for dinner tonight is such a problem. There is no single correct answer, but many possible answers. To be sure, some are less expensive than others (finishing the leftovers versus going out), some are more attractive than others (chicken versus green bean casserole), and some may be healthier (a salad versus a double cheese hamburger). When there are multiple possible solutions, we engage in divergent thinking, in coming up with various possible solutions. Thus divergent thinking is almost synonymous with creativity.

A Starting Point

We could spend a lot of time going over a number of definitions of creativity that "experts" have developed, only to find that there are many viewpoints and many disagreements about the nature of creativity. Let me, however, not do that and propose as a starting point a simple definition borrowed from a psychologist named Don MacKinnon.

MacKinnon believed that, in order to understand and usefully define creativity, one needs to look at actual behavior, at responses people make, rather than talk about the unconscious, Muses whispering in your ear, the historical impact of an invention, the abstract process by which discoveries are made, and so on.

MacKinnon postulated that a response is creative if it fulfills these three conditions:

1. The response must be original or novel. By this, he meant "statistically infrequent." If I ask you what your name is, a reply of "George" or "Maria" is not an original response. Most people, when asked for their name, reply with a name. But if you replied "1492," that would be novel or "statistically infrequent." Similarly, if a high school teacher assigns the task of writing a poem about love, references to Romeo and Juliet, Valentine's Day, or carving one's initials on a tree trunk would probably occur with some frequency. Poems based on two submarines sharing adjacent docks would be less likely, and therefore novel. Note that novel responses could simply be bizarre, the result of a mentally ill mind, a lie, or a misunderstanding. Just meeting this one condition does not equal creativity, but it is a beginning.

2. The response must fulfill the requirements of the situation—it must be adaptive. For example, the suggestion that declaring the use of money illegal could solve our country's economic problems would not be adaptive. Similarly, if I go to an architect to have her design a three-bedroom home, and she designs a magnificent cathedral, in that context her response would not fulfill this condition. Saying that one's name is "1492" might be original, but not adaptive and, hence, using MacKinnon's definition, not creative.

3. The response must be developed, must be realized. It is not sufficient to have in the back of one's head the outline of the Great American novel. One must write it (or use a ghostwriter). If you come up with an idea for a better mousetrap, you have to build it or get someone to build it for you. The resulting response, whether a novel or a mousetrap, would then be creative. MacKinnon used a story to illustrate this point. A man dies and goes to heaven. He is being shown around by Saint Peter, who points to another person and says, "That's the greatest general that has ever lived." The man is puzzled and says, "That can't be. I knew him when he was alive, and he was a cobbler." Saint Peter replies, "Yes, you're right, but if he had been a general he would have been the greatest general of all time." In judging whether a response is creative, we need to focus on its actual existence, not on wishes or unrealized intentions. Notice, then, that at the very minimum creativity involves two crucial aspects. First, the creative ideas must be generated—that light bulb in the mind must go on. But, secondly, the creative ideas must be implemented, must be given life.

4. To the three conditions listed above, I like to add a fourth, and that is the notion of "elegant simplicity." It seems to

me that most, if not all, creative responses are marked by both elegance and simplicity—in fact, we often respond to a creative product with "Why didn't I think of that!" If you are familiar with Picasso's painting of the dove, it is poetically beautiful and very simple, with some viewers saying, "A fifth grader could have done that." But it took Picasso's genius and talent to produce such a painting. Similarly, if you look at the kitchen appliances you have, like the "panini press" or the George Foreman grill, the pet rock or the Rubik's cube phenomenon of some years ago—all these have both an elegance and a simplicity to them. Even Einstein's theory of relativity can be said to have both!

Stanley Martin Lieber was born in New York City in 1922, the son of Jewish Romanian immigrants. Their mother treated both Stanley and his brother with much love, but the father was quite strict. In all fairness, times were very difficult for the family, with the Great Depression of 1929, as well as the loss of a considerable amount of money in a failed business; frequent family arguments and paternal strictness probably reflected this. Stanley retreated into reading everything he could get ahold of, as well as going to the local movie theater and listening to radio comedians like Jack Benny. During high school, Stanley participated in many school activities, developed into a gifted writer, and exhibited a good sense of humor. He eventually obtained a job as personal assistant to the art director of a comic book company called Timely Publications. This was a good time to be in the comic book industry, as Superman had just been introduced to the public by another company, and had been followed by Captain America, invented by the owner of Timely Publications.

Stanley was both ambitious and talented, and his boss recognized this and gave Stanley opportunities to display both. In 1941 Stanley decided to change his name to Stan Lee. After a career in the military and a subsequent marriage, Lee started his own publishing company—Madison Publications. He wrote a number of books that consisted of photographs (for example, of political leaders) with satirical captions. He also kept writing for Timely Publications, which eventually morphed into Marvel Comics. One day, Lee saw a fly crawling on the wall, and he was inspired to develop a comic book character with the power to stick to a wall like an insect. This was the birth of Spider-Man. The initial story involved a teenager, Peter Parker, who, bitten by a radioactive spider, develops the strength and acrobatic abilities of a spider. (Miller, 2006)

A Creative Problem-Solving Model

Perhaps MacKinnon's model seems too simplistic for you: a good beginning, but you want something more meaty that you can sink your teeth into, something that seems a bit more "academic." A theoretical model that has been quite useful is the Creative Problem-Solving Model developed by Parnes (1981) and based on Osborn (1953). The model consists of five stages, and in each stage there is, first, a phase of generating as many ideas as possible, and then a second phase of evaluating these ideas and creating a smaller list of potentially useful ideas. These are the five stages:

1. Fact-finding. When journalists write a newspaper column, they are taught to use the questions, "who, what, when, where, why, and how." Similarly, at this stage, the

problem solver (you) is asked to consider the above six questions. This is very similar to what we will learn later as the preparation stage. So, for example, if you are asked at work to consider ways in which the company can save money, you might wonder:

a. Who in the company should be involved in this process?
b. What are some of the ways the company has already tried to save money?
c. When does the company need to save money?
d. Where does the company need to save money?
e. Why does the company need to save money?
f. How does the company need to save money?

There are of course, other questions that can be asked, such as:

a. Who is an expert on saving money?
b. Who controls the flow of money in the company?
c. Who likes to spend money?
d. Who can be useful in promoting a plan to save?
e. Who has already done this at some other company?

The intent, here, is to generate a large number of ideas that reflect the factual basis of the challenge to be solved. Each idea may or may not serve to identify crucial components, resource people, alternate ways to think of the problem, and maybe even potential solutions. The same set of questions can be asked of serious challenges (how can we save Jim's life with a liver transplant?), or more mundane concerns (what will I serve for dinner tonight?).

2. PROBLEM-FINDING. How a problem is defined often determines the kind of solution one comes up with. For example, if I think that my teenage son is showing disrespect towards me as an authority figure, I might come up with a number of solutions that are punitive in nature. If I think his disrespect is really a way of showing independence, I might think of solutions that involve healthier ways for him to practice that independence. If I think his behavior is really a reaction to my being too tyrannical, then a different set of solutions might ensue.

So, in this stage of problem-solving, the focus is on developing a list of different ways in which the initial problem can be stated. In the first example above, is the concern really saving money or one of cash flow? Perhaps the problem is one of lax bookkeeping or of generating more money. Or perhaps it might be beneficial for the company's objectives to actually be spending more money.

Here, again, a list of potential ways of defining and redefining the problem is generated, and then these are analyzed logically to determine which ones make the most sense.

3. IDEA-FINDING. Suppose that in stage 2 we re-define the initial problem from "How can the company save money?" to "How can we stop paying the exorbitant interest rates on the company's debts?" In this third stage, we now generate as many ideas as possible without evaluation or criticism. For example, we might think of switching banks, getting a new loan at a new rate, discussing the problem with the manager of the bank, declaring bankruptcy, selling the company to a competitor, having each employee contribute a sum to pay off the debt, and so on. This stage is really one of brainstorming (see page 99).

4. Solution-finding. Here, we develop a list of criteria against which the solutions generated in stage 3 can be evaluated. Such criteria might be: Is what we are proposing legal? Will the CEO be amenable to this solution? Is the solution ethical? Can it be accomplished in the required time framework? And so on. Then each of the solutions from stage 3 is evaluated against these criteria, and the best solutions are selected.

5. Idea-implementation. In this stage, a plan of action is formulated—that is, what needs to be done to take this solution and make it happen.

We need to keep in mind that this sequence of stages is not rigid. In real life problem-solving, there may be considerable going back and forth, or even skipping of stages. But, for now, we can consider this model a useful map that shows how to get from a vague or specific challenge to the implementation of a creative solution.

Creative Thinking

The above approach focuses on creativity as a way of thinking, so we need to take a bit of a closer look at thinking and, specifically, at the many dimensions of thinking. Psychologists don't agree on how many dimensions there are to creative thinking, but these seem to be the most commonly mentioned:

1. Fluency: the ability to produce many ideas or responses. For example, how many names of animals can you list that begin with the letter p?

2. Flexibility: the ability to give responses that are in different categories. For example, name as many round objects as you can. If you said, "Basketball, soccer ball, baseball, and bowling ball," you would be scored low in flexibility. If you said, "A pearl, a drop of mercury, a

coffee bean, a marble," you would be equal in fluency (four responses), but higher in flexibility.

3. ORIGINALITY: We saw this in MacKinnon's criteria of creativity. Originality can be defined as infrequent, unique, not common, and these aspects can actually be measured by considering the responses of a large group of individuals. Thus, in a free association test (what comes to mind when I say the word ___), a response of "chair" to the word "table" would not be original, but the response "paper clip" would be. Note, again, that originality by itself could be bizarre or nonsensical.

4. ELABORATION: the ability to embellish, to add details. For example, two persons are each given a drawing of a circle and instructed to draw a face. One person might make a smiley face by adding eyes and a mouth. The second person, higher in elaboration, might add ears, a nose, some hair, a hat, earrings, perhaps a pirate's patch, a neck and necktie, and a large black mole on the left cheek. The number of elaborations would be independent of any artistic skill.

5. VISUALIZATION: the ability to see something in one's "mind's eye," for example, to visualize how you might hold your golf club or tennis racket in a game. Visualization also involves the ability to manipulate and alter such images. Imagine a black dog. Now change the color of that dog to green. Now make the green dog do a "hand" stand. If you can do that, you are probably quite good at visualization.

6. TRANSFORMATION: How good are you at changing one idea into another? When you cook "spaghetti squash" can you really think of those strands as spaghetti? Can you look at a file of soldiers and see wieners instead? Can you think of toothpaste as a flowing river? It can be

argued that much of creativity involves a transformation, a changing of one idea into another, an old object into a new, improved object, and a common use into an uncommon use.

7. Problem orientation: Perhaps you have had the opportunity to work with someone who seemed to have an uncanny ability to identify problems, to simplify them, to separate the chaff from the wheat, to propose alternative ways to define a particular problem. That person had a high "problem orientation"—not in the bad sense that he or she found problems where there were none, but in the good sense that, when a problem or challenge arose, they were able to deal with it effectively.
8. Analytical thinking: the ability to separate a problem into its components, to break a whole into its parts.
9. Synthesis: refers to the thinking ability to combine parts into a whole, to perceive how parts that may appear disparate are actually interrelated.
10. Regression in the service of the ego: a rather complex psychoanalytic term, but, in a very simplistic way, it means going back to childhood ways of thinking. Children can be very curious, can ask a lot of questions (as any parent knows), can challenge what, to an adult, is a logical assumption (Why can't I jump from the roof on my Pogo stick?), can disregard the rules of a game, and can be very self-centered.
11. Novelty: How alert is a person to something novel? How well can the person cope with novelty? What happens when you suggest to a friend, "Let's do lunch at that new restaurant" or "Let's try the new Japanese breadcrumbs that everyone is talking about"? Is your friend's first response one of hesitation or one of "No, let's do our usual"?

There are many more dimensions of thinking, but for our purposes these are enough. Obviously, the dimensions listed above are not independent of each other, nor are they separate from personality, attitudes, and other aspects of human functioning.

THE FOUR P'S OF CREATIVITY

Psychologists who study creativity approach the topic from one of four viewpoints. (1) The creative *person* (e.g., what characteristics do people like Mozart, DaVinci, and Einstein share? Do creative people talk, dream, and think differently from the rest of the population? Are creative people a little crazy? Or maybe a lot crazy? Are they amoral or immoral? Is their family background different?). (2) The creative *process* (e.g., are there steps or stages that one goes through when creating? What happens when a painter creates a painting? What happens when that inner light bulb goes on in the head of an inventor? By what process does the poet weave his/her visual tapestries?). (3) The creative *product* (e.g., what distinguishes a creative from a pedestrian painting? Are there certain qualities of balance, asymmetry, form, and motion that are part and parcel of a creative product?). (4) The creative *press* (e.g., what aspects of the environment facilitate or hinder creativity?). Note that environment here includes both the external environment (e.g., do classroom walls painted blue enhance creative behavior?), and the internal environment (e.g., how does motivation enhance or inhibit creativity?).

THE FOUR STAGES OF THE CREATIVE PROCESS

What happens when you are faced with a challenge that can require a creative solution? Or, to put it another way, what happens during the creative process? There are several answers to this question, but one that has stood the test of time considers the creative process to be made up of four stages:

1. PREPARATION. Imagine a gardener who wants to plant a tree. What will that person do? He or she will need to determine what kind of tree is to be planted, where it will be purchased, where it will be planted, if a permit is required, how large a hole will need to be dug, if the tools are available, if this is a one-person job or if help will be needed, if there is a convenient source of water, if the tree will need to be protected from rabbits or deer until it is established, and so on. A lot of preparatory work needs to be done. Similarly, a creative solution requires much preparatory work.

   The aim of this stage of preparation is to gather lots of data, lots of ideas, lots of potential bits of information that may or may not be relevant. To do this well, you must be open to new ideas and new information, and you must not be judgmental. There are several aspects that can get in the way here, and one must be sensitive to them:

   a. Habits. Like old shoes, they are very comfortable and, therefore, there is a tendency to reject new shoes. Thus, old ideas, old ways of doing something are more comfortable, and it is easy to reject new ways.

      A shoe is a shoe, and we rarely think of it as a hammer, unless we're driven to exasperation because we don't have a hammer. This is what psychologists call "functional fixedness"—once we learn the function of something (shoes are for wearing on feet), that function is fixed, and alternate ways of using that object are not easily obtained.

   b. Self-criticism. We are too quick to judge that an idea "will not work," that "my boss will think I'm incompetent," or "that's too obvious—if it worked, somebody would already have tried it."

c. Lack of tenacity. Most of us do not have the tenacity, the persistence to keep at something. When we read about creative people, inventors who finally achieved a breakthrough, we find that a common theme is that they worked very hard for long periods of time; they did not give up their quest simply because others said "you're crazy" or "you'll never achieve that goal," or because they felt the anguish of defeat, the frustration of beating their head against what seemed like a solid wall of failure. It has been said that genius is 1% inspiration and 99% perspiration, and there is much truth in that. Most creative insights are surrounded by a tremendous amount of discipline, hard work, knowledge of one's field, and continued effort, both before the creative insight and after.

The Story of Post-it Notes

You are most likely familiar with those yellow (and now multicolored, as well) notes called Post-it notes. They were not developed on purpose, but were the result of a failure and an observation. The story begins with Spencer Silver, a 3M scientist who was trying to develop a very strong adhesive, but failed and developed a very weak adhesive instead. There was not much of a market for something that didn't work, but Silver did not set the weak glue aside. For over five years, he gave seminars on the chemical structure of his discovery and tried his best to get his company interested in doing something with this highly unusual adhesive. Four years later, Arthur Fry, another 3M scientist, was having trouble keeping markers in his hymnal book. He was a choir member, and his many bookmarks kept falling out. He remembered

Silver's adhesive and used some on his bookmarks. Not only did they stay in place, but also they could easily be removed without damaging the hymnal pages. Not unexpectedly, Fry was an intensely curious person and an "inventor" (as a child in Iowa, he would take scrap pieces of lumber and turn them into custom-designed toboggans). He had also attended one of Silver's seminars and had been impressed by the adhesive. He therefore proposed a product that was essentially a bookmark. You would think that the notion of Post-it notes would have been fully embraced by the company, but it was not. There was a lot of skepticism—after all, why would people pay for a product that could easily be made from scraps of paper? The development of this product was almost "killed" by management, but fortunately Fry was tenacious. Some ten years after Silver's "failure," 3M began distributing Post-it notes (in 1980). They are now one of the most popular office products.

These preparatory aspects (specific techniques will be presented later) will help focus on some potential creative solutions, but quite often the result is that no viable creative solutions are generated. So the second stage takes place.

EXERCISE FOR PREPARATORY STAGE. A local company manufactures a product we will call the XY widget. Sales of these widgets have fallen substantially in the past six months. You are hired to come up with some creative solutions to this problem. What are some of the questions and information you would like to have? For example, you might want to know what the XY widget is—whether it is an automobile or a screwdriver might make a difference. What else?

2. INCUBATION. Popularly, this is akin to the idea of "sleep on it." The person turns away from consciously focusing on a solution and engages in other activities, like sleeping, playing a game of tennis, answering e-mail, going for a walk, etc. Obviously, if the challenge you are facing is really important (your job and/or your marriage depends on it), you are not going to be able to "forget" the challenge and play tennis as if you had no worries—so, in reality, it is somewhat questionable whether incubation really takes place. But at a superficial level, at least, this stage represents a turning away from the problem. As we will see, dreams are of particular importance at this stage, as well as the altering of everyday consciousness. Incubation is like the first three months of pregnancy. From outside there is very little to notice—it's a quiescent time. But, inside, a lot of activity and growth is going on.

3. ILLUMINATION. If the second stage is successful, then at this third stage the light bulb in the brain turns on. One or several solutions are perceived, often in a rather sudden and emotionally charged fashion. This stage is also called the "Aha!" stage. If you have ever experienced a sudden understanding, you will recognize this stage.

   EXAMPLE OF ILLUMINATION. Many years ago, I had been wrestling for some time with a research study I wanted to carry out (as a young assistant professor it was indeed "publish or perish"). The research design I wanted to use had several flaws, but I could not perceive a way around them. Then I went to Montreal for a psychological convention. I walked into a church (I believe it was Notre Dame) that was quite empty. I sat down and my mind wandered to the research problem I had been wrestling with. Suddenly, I saw the solution before my eyes and heard some very loud organ music. I looked at the choir loft and the organ, but there was no one there. The music and the solution were in my head, but as clear and vivid as if I had been attending a concert.

4. Verification. Unfortunately, "Aha!" experiences can turn out to be duds: incorrect, not implementable, not practical, or simply not acceptable to other folks (remember the Edsel automobile!). So, in this verification stage, the creative insight needs to be assessed; a reality check needs to be made. Brilliant insights must be laboriously elaborated into a finished product. Perhaps Mozart did hear finished symphonies in his head, but most likely he wrestled with them and wrote and rewrote, revised and re-revised, as most composers do.

These stages are generic and simplistic, like a stick drawing of a house. They may or may not match a particular situation, but in general represent a fairly good map of what often happens on the way to a creative solution. Sometimes, stages are skipped (we don't always need to "sleep on it"), and sometimes a solution that turns out to be a dud in the verification stage results in several potential creative solutions that, indeed, may work.

Can Creativity Be Taught?

Obviously, we cannot take just any group of children and turn them into future Einsteins, Mozarts, or Picassos. Even though, historically, some educators believed that the mind was a "tabula rasa," a blank tablet, and that the appropriate education could result in either a genius or a thief, we now realize that not only is the human mind extremely complex—a result of learning experiences plus genetics, physiology, nutrition, parental expectations, peer influences, etc.—but the world is also complex, as is the very nature of creativity.

If we are somewhat more modest in our goals, then, yes, we can teach people to be more creative, more sensitive to their environment, more curious, more alert, more aesthetically sensitive, more reflective, and more self-actualizing.

When I was an undergraduate student at a small Catholic university, I had the opportunity to meet the Director of the Alumni office. Ordinarily, our two paths should not have crossed, but they did. He was actually a former English professor and took me under his wing. He gave me paperback books to read; at that time, paperbacks were only found in drugstores and had a somewhat sleazy quality to them, dominated by Westerns (Zane Grey) and detective stories (Mickey Spillane). We would meet together under a tree in the California sunshine, and he would point out how the beginning sentence of a book tried to captivate my interest, or how a character was developed throughout a story. We would discuss how a Western was similar to the Greek masterpieces like *The Iliad*, or how Mickey Spillane was relevant to my struggles as a young adult. I learned more from him than from any regularly scheduled class, and developed a great appreciation for reading and writing.

The Apprenticeship Model

When we think of "education," we usually think of a school, or a formal setting. But much of what we learn is discovered outside of the classroom, especially when we think of knowledge related to our jobs. In many professions, as well as artisan endeavors, the apprenticeship model is still very much with us. Physicians do internships, a residency, and sometimes even more specialized training under the guidance of others. New architects do a long period of apprenticeship with more established architects. Rookie police officers are often teamed up with more senior partners. Glass blowers study at the elbow of well-known blowers, and so on. Often, those of us who are not required to do such an apprenticeship will read about well-known figures in our chosen field in hopes of learning something from these master achievers. So, if you want to be creative and apprenticing yourself is not possible, reading about highly creative people can provide useful information.

> In a magazine advertisement for American Express, Martin Scorsese, the exceptionally talented film director, is asked who gives him inspiration and replies, "Other filmmakers."

Michael Gelb wrote an interesting book titled *How to Think Like Leonardo DaVinci*. Gelb feels that the hallmark of DaVinci's genius consists of seven steps or principles, and that these can, to some degree, be taught to individuals who want to enhance their creative abilities. Here are the seven steps with the Italian labels that Gelb uses:

1. "CURIOSITA" or curiosity, as exemplified by a high degree of curiosity towards the world, an appetite for continuous learning.

2. "DIMOSTRAZIONE" or focus on doing. Gelb and others have argued that experience is the source of wisdom. So "dimostrazione" has to do with a focus on knowledge through experience, on making mistakes but learning from them, on persistence and tenacity.

3. "SENSAZIONE" or using one's senses. The focus here is on relating to the world through the senses—for example, being alert and sensitive to color nuances, being aware of details, using not only sight, which for most of us is the primary sense, but also touch and hearing, and even intuition.

4. "SFUMATO". This Italian word comes from the word "fumo," which means smoke. In Italian, "fumare" means to smoke, and a "sfumatura" refers to the shades and tones in a painting that are not clearly defined, but have a smoke-like quality. By using this beautifully poetic word, Gelb points to the ability to tolerate ambiguity, to be comfortable with uncertainty, to be able to hold two or more opposing ideas without the need to make a judgment as to which one is correct and which is not.

5. "ARTE/SCIENZA". DaVinci was both an artist and a scientist. He studied rocks and plants and human anatomy and many other areas, and was able to express his insights and findings in detailed drawings. He was *the* Renaissance man, the "whole brain" thinker, blessed with the capacity to use both the right side of the brain and the left side.

6. "CORPORALITA". "Corpo" is the Italian word for body, and a study of DaVinci's life suggests that he was also blessed with a strong physique, had the ability to be ambidextrous, and was an athletic individual with great poise and grace. If you have these attributes, you are lucky, indeed, particularly since our culture (like most cultures) places a premium on them. If you don't have these attributes, act as if you did—sometimes that works! Obviously, there are also ways that a person can, to some degree, increase the strength of their physique, or their poise. But, in terms of creativity, this is probably the least important. After all, what kind of physique did Toulouse-Lautrec have?!

7. "CONNESSIONE" or connectivity. DaVinci appreciated that the world is not made of disparate elements, but that

there are patterns, analogies, and connections. He wrote that swimming in water could teach one how birds fly in the air.

The problem with Gelb's book, as excellent as it is, is that reading about DaVinci and the seven dimensions that defined his genius is both exhilarating and discouraging. He was, after all, a unique individual, far above the rest of us mere mortals!

William Powell Lear was born in Hannibal, Missouri in 1902. He was an extremely bright youngster with a very unstable mother. She kept walking out on her husband and taking William along; she then lived with a series of men until she found a more or less permanent relationship. She was an angry woman who took her frustrations out on her son, beating him and hurling vicious insults at him. When he was eleven, the family moved to Chicago, and William immersed himself in books and technology. By the time he was twelve, he had built himself a radio receiver and a telegraph. He dropped out of high school in his freshman year and began hanging around the local airport. He served six months in the Navy and tried a number of jobs. He married, but his marriage ended in divorce, due to his infidelity.

By age twenty-six he had invented a miniaturized coil to be used in radios and devised a radio to be installed in cars; this radio was called "Motorola." An additional invention (eliminating the bulky battery that the car radio needed and using instead the low-voltage current from the car's battery) turned the Motorola radio into a great success, and the entire company was named Motorola. But William abandoned Motorola, despite the promise of great financial rewards, and turned his attention to his true love: airplanes. William Powell Lear established his company, Lear Inc., and was greatly aided by the Second World War and its demand for instruments for warplanes. He was both successful and near bankruptcy a number of times. He was married and a womanizer. Above all, he was an inventor, a mechanical genius, who saw opportunities where others saw defeat. Eventually, he took a Swiss military jet and turned it into the ultimate status symbol—a personal jet plane. The Lear jet company became well known, as did Bill Lear. Lear died of leukemia in 1978 at age seventy-five. (Heppenheimer, 1989)

Keeping Our Perspective

Creativity is like sex. It is wonderful, exhausting, and energizing, but, despite what some people believe, it is only a small segment of our daily lives. Creativity (in most cases…) does not pay the rent, it does not prepare our food, it does not keep our cars running and our airplanes flying. Life would be highly chaotic if it were not for the routine, non-creative, but necessary activities we all engage in. Every time I fly in an airplane, I fervently pray that the pilot is more of a compulsive person than a creative one! Creativity is like the sauce on a filet mignon; it is what makes the filet mignon so delicious, but it is the filet mignon that provides the sustenance—the iron and the calories. At the same time, a world without creativity is like a world without color. Would we survive in a drab, gray, foggy type of environment? Of course, but it would be a very sad existence, akin to being severely depressed (please, no comments about the British…). Whatever else creativity may be, remember that it is a skill and, like any skill, you need to practice, practice, practice.

> Even at age fifty-eight, Twyla Tharp, a well-known choreographer and professional dancer, felt the need to dance every day. She stated, "You don't get into the mood to create—it's discipline." Faith Ringgold, an art Professor at the University of California at San Diego, gets up around four o'clock in the morning in order to have sufficient time for her creative work. Janet Evanovich, the creator of the adventures of New Jersey bounty hunter Stephanie Plum, wakes up at 5 AM and writes until 1 PM.

Fantasy vs. Reality

Although much of creativity involves fantasy—the dreams that initiate a creative solution, the what-if playfulness of creative innovation, the whispering of the Muses—there is also a very realistic component. By this, I mean that the creative person is not satisfied with generating ideas, but wants to see those translated into real life events, whether that involves publishing a book of poetry, building a new civic center, or trying out a different way of preparing cole slaw. Part of this reality component also involves determining whether the creative idea or innovative insight will, in fact, work.

The popular image of what creativity is all about is at variance with the reality. Sometimes, people think that creative writers do nothing but sit around a bar table on the left bank of the Seine river and by "osmosis" imbibe from their creative surroundings the wine of inspiration. In fact, most creative individuals work very hard at their creating. They not only have the passion and enthusiasm, but also are willing to work very hard—indeed, love to do so. At the same time, remember there is no such thing as "creative people" versus the rest of the world. Everyone is potentially creative, and everyone can use assistance.

> Stan Freberg, the comedian and satirist, described himself as a procrastinator and felt he needed deadlines in order to be productive. Similarly, Bobby McFerrin, the "Don't worry, be happy" singer (who was also an excellent composer, conductor, and first-class musician) stated that he needs to set a goal or a deadline in order to get anything done.

Do the Muses Really Whisper?

A popular view of creativity, unfortunately reinforced by some highly creative people, as well as some "experts" who ought to know better, is that creativity is a mysterious process that we mere mortals cannot hope to understand. This process involves phenomena out of our reach—like the Muses whispering in our ear, God speaking directly to a favorite son like Mozart, or unconscious processes bubbling up and erupting, like a hearty burp, into consciousness.

Perhaps Mozart had the unusual gift of seeing in his mind's eye a finished composition before he wrote it on paper, but that doesn't mean the Muses were whispering in his ear. We can consider creativity very much like intelligence—everyone, even the most profoundly retarded individual, has some intelligence. How much intelligence an individual has is the result of the interplay of genetics, anatomy, biochemistry, physiology, environment, learning, motivation, and myriad other aspects—complicated, yes, but potentially understandable. Creativity can be and has been studied, it can be and has been taught, and it can be sustained.

An experiment done many years ago is relevant here. A psychologist presented a number of subjects with the following problem: there were two strings hanging from the ceiling that were to be tied together. The difficulty was that the two strings were at a distance from each other such that they could not be grasped at the same time. A solution was to set one of the strings in motion like a pendulum, grasp the second string, and then the pendulum string could also be grasped, as it swung closer. Most of the subjects did not solve the problem even after ample time. The experimenter then walked by, "accidentally" brushing one of the strings and setting it in motion. This was an effective hint that helped quite a few subjects to solve the problem. When the experimenter asked if anything had helped the subject solve the problem, about half of the subjects made no mention of the "accidental" hint. They simply reported that the solution had "popped" into their head.

The Gillette Razor

The Gillette razor and its disposable blades were invented by King Camp Gillette (yes, that was really his name). He was born in 1855 in Fond du Lac, Wisconsin, into a family of inventors. His father was in the hardware business and the holder of several patents. His mother was co-author of *The White House Cook Book*, a best-seller, and she continually experimented with recipes. In the late 1800's, Gillette was a bottle cap salesman. The president of the company had invented a cork-lined bottle cap: the "Crown cork." He told Gillette to try to invent something like the Crown cork—an inexpensive, disposable item. Gillette became obsessed with the idea. One day, as he was starting to shave and realized that the blade on his razor was dull, inspiration hit. As he later wrote: "I saw it all in a moment, and in that same moment many unvoiced questions were asked and answered more with the rapidity of a dream than by the slow process of reasoning..." In those days razors lasted a lifetime, though their blades needed to be stropped and honed on a daily basis. Most men preferred to go to a barber for their shaves.

It took Gillette from 1895 to 1903 to produce a working razor and blades, and he needed the help of another inventor, William Emery Nickerson. In the first year of production, Gillette sold 51 razors and 168 blades. By 1904, his company had sold 91,000 razors and more than 2 million blades! (Mansfield, 1992)

WHERE DO CREATIVE IDEAS COME FROM?

The quick answer is "everywhere." Creative ideas are all around us, like viruses, and sometimes they "invade" our brains despite our best effort to keep them out. We can, of course, also train ourselves to become more sensitive, more receptive to potentially creative ideas. Most likely, you have had the experience of living in a town or city and never noticing the luggage repair shop down the street until you needed your luggage repaired. Some creative ideas are just like the luggage repair shop—unseen and unused until the need arises. So, if you're wrestling with a problem that might need a creative solution, pay attention to your world, and the need you have may trigger the perception of "luggage repair shops" all around you.

In contrast to the above, which basically has to do with the "muses whispering in your ear" (more simply, a matter of awareness) or that cauldron of ideas and feelings called the unconscious, bubbling up some ideas like gas going north instead of south, there is the directed approach, the conscious attempt to generate creative ideas, as in brainstorming (see page 99).

Sometimes, too, creative ideas occur because of chance or good luck—the so-called serendipity aspect. For example, the inventor of basketball was trying to develop an indoor sport that could be played in a gym. He asked a janitor to get him some boxes, but the poor fellow could only find some peach baskets, and the sport of basketball, rather than box-ball, was born.

All of us are familiar with bar codes, those ubiquitous sets of black bars found on practically every item in a grocery store, as well as luggage tags, library books, items for sale in department stores, and a million other places. The first use of such a bar code in the grocery field occurred in 1974 in an Ohio supermarket, but the bar code was invented in 1949 by Joe Woodland, an engineer.

Mr. Woodland wanted to invent an automated checkout procedure for supermarkets, since the manual ringing up of prices was slow and prone to a lot of errors. He went down to the beach, sat on a beach chair and started thinking about the challenge. He realized that he needed a code, but the only code he knew was the Morse code he had learned as a Boy Scout. As he thought about the Morse code, he ran his fingers through the sand and looked at the four furrows his hand had made. AHA! He realized that he could encode information in the form of wide and narrow lines, just as Morse had encoded the letters of the alphabet into dots and dashes.

Creativity As Personality

We can think of creativity, from the perspective of personality, as a set of characteristics allowing a person to act in a particular way. For example, we consider some people to be extroverted—they are outgoing, friendly, often talkative. In the same manner, we consider some people to have creative personalities—they are accepting of themselves and others, they are original and inventive (but not necessarily "talented"), they are genuine and spontaneous, independent, often exhibit a good sense of humor, they are not prejudiced in the usual sense of the word, and they seem to have what the French call "joie de vivre"—a zest for life.

A well-known psychologist, Abraham Maslow, called them "self-actualized" people: people who live their lives to their full potential. If one defines creativity this way, then it becomes clear that one can live a full, actualized life without necessarily having the kind of talents exhibited by a Picasso, a DaVinci, or an Einstein. And, similarly, one can have the talents required to create a marvelous symphony or paint highly unusual masterpieces without being well-adjusted—think of Salvador Dali!

Deborah Henson-Conant has been described by Doc Severinson as "the wild woman of the harp." She was born in California in 1953, and is a highly creative musician who has taken an ancient instrument and turned it into an innovative spectacle. An article in *The Boston Globe* described her as "a combination of Leonard Bernstein, Steven Tyler, and Xena the Warrior Princess." She has toured with the Boston Pops, has played with various artists and orchestras, and has garnered a number of awards.

Deborah writes that, when she was about five, she discovered that family plus time together equaled music. She describes her mother as a "Grocery Store Diva," who belted out songs while shopping. She learned to play the ukulele when she was seven, and by age thirteen she could accompany her mom's singing on the piano. If you want a glimpse of her creativity, attend one of her concerts or read her essay, "The Reluctant Non-Stepmother," at www.hipharp.com.

Chapter 2

The Building Blocks of Creativity

By now, you realize that creativity is not a single "thing," a unitary phenomenon, but rather complex and made up of many components. For many who study creativity, the question of how many components exist is a favorite one, and various numbers have been proposed. Let's leave that issue to the professionals and, instead, look at what seem to be the major components of creativity.

Curiosity

Creativity is like a plant that needs good soil, food, water, and sunshine to grow. The entire climate needs to be appropriate for the needs of a particular plant. For creativity the climate is curiosity. You need to wonder:

"What if...?"
"How does this work?"
"What happens when...?"
"Why...?"
"Is this really true?"

Almost everyone is familiar with "Braille," a system of embossed type used by blind individuals to read with their fingertips. Louis Braille, who was born in 1809 near Paris, invented the system. When he was four years old, Louis lost his eyesight in one eye due to a horrible accident with an awl, and subsequently lost his other eye to an infection from his first eye.

At age ten, he entered a school for blind boys in Paris. Here, the children were taught practical skills, as well as how to read using letters that were raised above the surface of the paper. It was a difficult procedure to learn, and one that required a manufacturing process beyond the capability of a single individual. The children who mastered this system could read, but none could write. In 1821, a soldier visited the school and talked about "night writing." Night writing involved the use of twelve dots in various combinations, and its purpose was to allow soldiers to communicate with each other in nighttime maneuvers without revealing their positions to the enemy. The method proved too complex for soldiers and was rejected. Louis Braille, however, realized the importance of this system for the blind, and spent a number of years experimenting and refining it to a six-dot format. This method is still used today all over the world.

Passion

One of the hallmarks of creative people is passion about what they are doing. Whether they are painting, designing new software, or thinking about an advertising campaign to sell a new product, they have an extreme, consuming involvement in that activity. If you've ever been so engrossed in reading a book that you missed lunch, then you've experienced that passion. If you've ever read a biography of someone like Mozart or Einstein or Picasso, you will have read about such passion. Ann Patchett, the award-winning author of *Bel Canto* and other books, states that, while typing her manuscripts, she often forgets to eat until a particular word reminds her that she is starving!

In the May 14, 2007 issue of *Time* magazine, the editors presented their annual list of the 100 most influential persons. Martin Scorsese, the well-known film director, describes Leonard DiCaprio, a very gifted young actor who has become a superstar. Scorsese tells of DiCaprio's commitment that is "fierce and total," and describes him as a "passionate student" who "never stops studying and learning." Other nominees included Brian Williams, the NBC nightly news anchor, who is described as having a "broad array of passions," and Simon Fuller, the creator of *American Idol*, who is a passionate fan of soccer and other sports.

Passion is often developed early in childhood, and whether the child is living in a musical family or playing with an erector set makes little difference. Unfortunately, our society does not reward passion. We prefer our children to be "well rounded," and we want adults to be on time for dinner and other social obligations.

The first question to ask, then, is whether there is passion in your life about something—hopefully, but not necessarily, related to your work. Do you love old airplanes and are you knowledgeable about them? Are you an "authority" on sports? Do you enjoy cooking and are you always searching for new recipes? Are you a birder? If there isn't something that you are passionate about now, could you develop that passion, that intense interest in a particular area of human endeavor? If you are a stockbroker, could you focus on the very concept of stocks? What are they? How did they come to be? How are they regulated? Who are the most successful people in your field? How did they get there? What leads to success? What needs to be changed? What improvements could be made? How do your counterparts in other countries carry out their activities? If you were to die and return 100 years from now, what would your job look like? What if "stockbroking" were declared illegal? What other activities would be invented to take the place of the stock market?

Along with passion there is the need for discipline. Creativity is not a haphazard process, but rather requires a very focused and intensive approach. Curtis Carlson, the CEO of a company called SRI International, makes the same point in a fascinating book titled *Innovation: The Five Disciplines for Creating What Customers Want.* He believes that innovation is the result of a highly disciplined process based on five steps or disciplines:

1. Carlson believes that you should select important challenges, not just interesting challenges (remember that his book is written for personnel in companies where the bottom line is profit).

2. Will customers want this innovation? Will it fulfill their needs?

3. Whoever is in charge of the project to carry out this innovation must be "insanely" committed to the project (see passion above!).

4. Although a single person can be an inventor, to truly innovate in a business environment requires a full team approach. (This can be seen in the vignette about Post-it notes [see page 26]).

5. These disciplines or steps need to be built into the organization and across organizations.

You probably recognize the name Goodyear as a company known for the manufacture of automobile tires. Charles Goodyear was extremely interested in rubber, and it became a central passion in his life. Others, too, were interested in rubber and, in fact, in the 1830's there was a rubber boom in the United States, with rubber used in toys, in commercial applications, and in a variety of products—even portable rubber bathtubs! The boom did not last very long, as it became clear that rubber had substantial limitations. The heat of summer softened it, and the cold of winter made it brittle and prone to cracking. Even exposure to air and light over a period of time caused rubber to decompose.

Goodyear started his career as a mechanic, dabbled with rubber valves, and became determined to make rubber a stable and dependable material. He eventually purchased a small rubber company in the vicinity of Boston. In 1839, Goodyear accidentally dropped a piece of rubber coated with sulfur on a hot stove. The rubber did not melt because of the sulfur—and the process of vulcanization was born. This was not merely an accident, but the result of a lifelong passion involving years of labor and experimentation. Goodyear was looking for an answer, and his years of searching and preparation made him realize that answer when it accidentally appeared before his eyes. Probably the same can be said of Mozart. He might have believed that melodies appeared before his eyes fully formed, but it was the passion in his life that played a major role.

> Who hasn't read *A is for Alibi* and the other progressively named alphabetical titles of Sue Grafton, another prolific and entertaining writer? Grafton rises every day at 5:42 AM to write in her orderly office. She believes we all have a dark side (anger, jealousy) to our nature, but that's where the passion is. She believes you should trust your instincts, your first impressions.

Aesthetic Interest

Most creative people describe themselves as "artistic," whether or not they have artistic skills. They are interested in art, music, poetry, the beauty of a sunset, or the majesty of a mountain range. Aesthetic interest can be cultivated, not only through classes on music appreciation, books on art, visits to galleries and museums, and so on, but also through habit. The next time you open a door, *look* at it. Spend a few seconds admiring the wood grain, the workmanship, and the sleekness of the hinges. When you see a new car, a dress, or a vase, don't judge them by their price, but how aesthetically pleasing they are—the beauty of their lines, their colorfulness, the feelings of awe and admiration they arouse in you.

Imagination is a Habit

Like a lot of human behavior, creativity is, in large part, a habit. The problem is that most of us, after childhood, do not get the opportunity to practice being creative. By and large, the educational system stifles creativity. Teachers are often quite ingenious in the craft activities they create for youngsters in the classroom. Walk into most classrooms, and you'll find all sorts of cutouts, pictures, artwork, etc., hanging on the walls. There will be seasonal displays, like paper leaves during the Fall season, but look at those leaves—they are perfect, well-shaped so as to be quite recognizable, with colors that mimic Mother Nature. This is not creativity; this is learning, which certainly has its place in the school. But what about creating square leaves, as they might exist in a mythical land where children govern and adults go to school? What about purple polka dot leaves, or black leaves? This is not an indictment of teachers; I happen to be one myself. There are a lot of teachers who are indeed creative, but the system demands knowledge, facts, and passing scores on achievement tests, and creativity and imagination often get lost.

So start imagining, start thinking creatively, don't judge yourself harshly—there are enough people out there eager to take on that job! Exercise your creativity, and soon it will become second nature.

> Michael Crichton has written a number of best-selling books, including *The Andromeda Strain*, *Jurassic Park*, *The Great Train Robbery*, and *Terminal Man*. Crichton was a very imaginative child who kept his younger brother and two younger sisters entertained with his make-believe, his imaginative playing, and his continuous creating. Perhaps it helped that his parents were "eccentric" and emphasized learning and family togetherness. Crichton studied at Harvard Medical School to be a physician, yet believes in auras and other "mystical" concerns. He reportedly would wake up at 4 AM to drive to his office, where he would work on his books till early evening.

MOTIVATION

Psychologists speak of extrinsic (or external) motivation and intrinsic (or internal) motivation. External motivation has to do with things like a paycheck, a bigger office, recognition by others, words of praise, etc. Inner motivation is a bit harder to define—it has to do with self-actualization, with becoming and doing one's best because that is (or can be) satisfying in itself. It has to do with passion and curiosity and experiencing the fun of creating.

Although both types of motivation are important, the generation of creative ideas is more closely related to internal motivation than external motivation. In fact, external motivation can be inimical to creativity. We think about what worked well in the past, what brought in the money or the recognition, and we try the same thing again and again. Notice how many movies have been made with "II" or "III" in the title; they may have been commercial successes, but most were not creative or original.

> Did you ever hear of Albert Hurwit, the classical composer? Probably not, because Hurwit is actually a radiologist, a physician who specializes in X-rays, and he does not read music. But his true love is music, so after twenty-five years in a successful radiology practice he retired and devoted himself to composing. He describes how he would wake up in the night and hear music—symphonic themes would bubble to the surface. When this happens, he puts on his headphones so as not to disturb his wife, and works through the night. In 2002, the Hartford Symphony Orchestra performed a composition of his on the same program as Tchaikovsky and Brahms!

NOT THE OPPOSITE OF LOGICAL

We can consider creativity as a type of intelligence or, more specifically, a type of thinking. There are many different kinds of thinking; we can engage in logical thinking, in concrete thinking, in conceptual thinking, in visual thinking, and so on. If we consider creativity as a type of thinking and realize that the brain typically works in a cohesive manner, then we can see creative thinking as working hand-in-hand with other types of thinking. That is, creativity is not the opposite of logical, rational thinking—but both are needed. The key here is that logical, rational thinking is particularly needed after we have used creative thinking to come up with potential solutions. Logical thinking can then help us to evaluate which of the many solutions we have generated are indeed more do-able, easier to implement, more likely to result in an acceptable product, etc.

Most likely you have used Sylvan Goldman's invention on a routine basis without thinking twice. Goldman, the owner of a supermarket chain in Oklahoma City, invented the shopping cart. In those days, supermarket customers used hand-carried baskets, but the drawback was that, as baskets were filled with groceries, they could become quite heavy. That would also limit the number and kind of items customers might purchase. Goldman was inspired to design a shopping cart on wheels by two wooden folding chairs in his office. He realized that the two chairs, mentally placed on top of each other, could provide space for two baskets, and with the addition of wheels, customers could easily buy lots of groceries. Goldman worked with his maintenance man, and the two together met a number of technical challenges; in 1940 he was finally awarded a patent. Like many other inventions however, the shopping cart was not readily embraced. Women thought it looked too much like a baby carriage, and men found them too "effeminate." Goldman however, was very inventive. He hired a number of people of both genders and various ages to "shop" in his stores and visibly use the shopping cart. Eventually, the carts became quite popular, and Goldman died (in 1984) a very rich man.

CREATIVITY AS ANALOGY

It's been said that "there's nothing new under the sun," and perhaps that is true. Certainly, when one looks at creative products, they often have a history of inspiration based on other people's ideas or previous products. For example, many movies are based on books. Broadway musicals are similarly often based on other works of art. For example, "Rent" is based on a classical Italian opera called "La Boheme," which in turn was based on some autobiographical stories. "Cats," another long-running musical, was based on a book of poems by T. S. Eliot. So, when you are creating something "new," don't be paralyzed by the fiction that creativity must be totally novel. Don't be afraid to look for inspiration in other people's work, in historical accounts, in what has gone before.

> Gutenberg's invention of the printing press was facilitated because of his attendance at a wine festival. For quite some time, Gutenberg had been interested in how wax seals, which were used to seal letters, could be imprinted with a mark. He could not however, quite figure out how a large number of such seals could be pressed down on a piece of paper simultaneously, thus creating a whole page of marks (i.e., sentences). He had the good fortune, however, of attending a wine festival and seeing a wine press in action. He realized that the same principle of a flat area to which a uniform force is applied could be used to create a printing press.

SYNECTICS

William J. J. Gordon, a talented and creative person whose occupations ran the gamut from schoolteacher to pig breeder, developed the system of "synectics," which is a "joining together of different and apparently irrelevant elements." Gordon believed that everyone uses analogies to solve problems, and his system of synectics was a way of formalizing this process. He and his colleagues published a number of workbooks designed to use analogies in problem solving. The synectics method has been instrumental in a substantial number of inventions, ranging from Pringles Potato Chips (the potato chips stacked in a can), to electric knives, the Kleenex space-saver box, and others.

Gordon (1961) pointed out that the synectic approach involves "making the strange, familiar," and the "familiar, strange." The first step basically means that the person or group needs to understand the problem. Gordon was writing primarily for a process involving artistic or technical inventions, but his theory has broader applications. So the first step in creative problem solving is to become familiar with the problem or creative challenge one is facing. It is not sufficient to want to create a painting or a poem about the horrors of war. Which war? All wars? What specific horrors? The killing of innocent children? The psychological pain suffered by the combatants? The physical and emotional price paid by maimed survivors? The atrocities committed by soldiers? The lying and posturing of politicians? The waste of resources that could be used for the betterment of mankind?

The second aspect, to "make the familiar strange," means to turn away from the commonplace, usual, rational approach to the problem (because it hasn't worked), and to look at the problem situation in a new light. How is this done? Through the use of analogies, and specifically the use of one of these types of analogies:

1. PERSONAL ANALOGIES. This basically involves becoming part of the creative challenge. For example, John Keats, a well-known poet, wrote that, in writing a particular poem, he leaped (in his imagination) headlong into the ocean, so he could become acquainted with the sounds

and the waves and the rocks. Albert Einstein wrote that he could identify both visually and with his muscles with certain mathematical principles. So, if you are trying to create a better light bulb, you become that light bulb.

2. Direct analogies. Here, the problem is compared directly to something else that shares some of the same characteristics. For example, if you were trying to design a better container for anchovies, you might ask what kind of containers holds sardines, or pickled beets, or sun-dried tomatoes in olive oil. The Pringles Potato Chips were the result of dealing with the challenge of how to package potato chips so that breakage would be minimal. It was noted that wet leaves pack snugly together without breakage, and perhaps the same could be done with potato chips.

3. Symbolic analogies. Here the analogy is a symbolic one—that is, the problem is compared to something that is a symbol. For example, in designing our package for anchovies, we want something sturdy that does not leak, but we also want something light that won't give the purchaser a backache when they lift the container. So our symbol becomes that of "soft-hardness" or hardy-softness, and might get us to think about tomatoes that often have an almost unsliceable peel, or tempered glass that does not break easily, or the type of mesh that Crusaders wore.

4. Fantasy analogies. Here the focus is on fantasy, on thinking about fantastic solutions. For example, in trying to come up with a better toothpaste, you might imagine one that changes flavors depending on the wishes of the user. So, if today I'm in the mood for mint-flavored toothpaste, that's what comes out of the tube. If, instead, I

would prefer bourbon-flavored toothpaste, that's exactly what I would get. Fantasy, yes, but it might lead to the potentially practical notion of a toothpaste dispenser coupled with a miniature lazy susan that might indeed dispense one of eighteen prepackaged flavors.

> Joy Mangano was thirty-three, divorced, and with three children under age seven. She was quite busy, and mopping the floor was not something she looked forward to, especially wringing out the mop in dirty water. She designed a "self-wringing" mop, and today she is president of a multi-million dollar company, and one of the stars of the Home Shopping Network.

Metaphorical Thinking

One type of thinking particularly crucial to creativity is metaphorical thinking. A metaphor is a figure of speech in which a word is used in place of another to show a likeness between the two. Essentially, it can be considered thinking with analogies. Metaphorical thinking is very pervasive in most, if not all, languages, and in many human activities. If you've ever gone into a hardware store to buy an electrical or a plumbing supply item, you will have learned that there are "male" and "female" electrical and plumbing parts. Similarly, if you read about cancer (or another major disease) you will learn that there is a "war" against cancer, and that patients are "victims." If you've used a phrase like "A man's home is his castle" or "He is a devil," you've used metaphors and metaphorical thinking. Usually, however, you have not gone far enough. For example, the "house equals castle" metaphor might lead you to think about what products, services, etc., a castle owner might need. Is there a market for moats? Of course, there is. I remember seeing a custom-built house where the swimming pool and fountains were linked in such a way that the house was basically an island surrounded by separate, but connected, waterways.

> A Japanese engineer by the name of Tashikatsu Kuwahata, who worked for the company, JVC, thought that wood would be the ideal material to make the sound cone for speakers. But it was impossible to shape a sheet of wood into a cone without the wood cracking and splintering. When a colleague commented out loud how a nearby restaurant was able to transform squid—a rubbery and tough substance—into tender morsels, Mr. Kuwahata took notice and realized that the amino acids in the Japanese rice wine not only softened squid, but could do the same to sheets of wood. In 2004, JVC began selling the first line of wood-cone speakers.

SENSITIVITY TO PROBLEMS

Part of being creative is to be sensitive to problems. This does not mean being a pessimist, ready to see black clouds all over the place, but rather being able to correctly identify what the real problem is, how to break down a problem into its components, how to prioritize these components (what needs to be solved first), and how to determine what information is missing.

So, if the initial challenge is "how do we increase the company's earnings," perhaps we need to be sensitive to the fact that the real problem might be one of cash flow, or excessive expenses, or company greed, and so on. We may realize that the challenge might have various components, not just increasing earnings but increasing capital gains, or funds for research and development, or contributions to political races, salaries of the employees, pension plans, etc. Each of these components might then be better treated separately.

If the challenge is to redecorate our room, we might want to break that challenge into subgroups and handle each of these separately. One approach might be to think of the activities that take place there: sleeping, studying, listening to music, surfing the internet, storing our clothes, making cappuccino, watching television, and entertaining our friends. Each of these can be handled individually, even though several of these will interface with each other.

Once a challenge has been identified, we can also ask if there are alternate ways to define the problem—for example, slow sales of a product might be reformulated in terms of brand recognition or cultural blocks. In the United States, drinking wine has become a fairly acceptable phenomenon. When you go to a grocery or liquor store to buy wine, you most likely purchase what you recognize: Merlot, Chianti, or Pinot Noir. It takes a real connoisseur to look for Brunello di Montalcino, Amarone, or Barbaresco.

Taking Risks

To be creative means to take risks, to make errors, to feel the anxiety of the unknown, to fear failure or ridicule by others. Think how often in your life these fears have guided your behavior. Perhaps a new ethnic restaurant opened up, but you were afraid of going in by yourself. Or, as you drive back and forth from home to work, you might consider going a different way, but the fear that you might get lost or be late prevents you from exploring an alternative.

Just as we have convergent thinking and divergent thinking, there are convergent thinkers and divergent thinkers—that is, people who prefer to accept a well-defined amount of information when faced with a problem, and those who are more comfortable with a rather broad amount of information. Thus, to solve the problem, "What is 4 x 4?", a convergent thinker only needs to know that 16 is the correct answer. A divergent thinker however, may have knowledge about imaginary numbers, set theory, algebraic equations, statistical probability, and so on, and may perceive, in addition to the "correct answer," several other possibilities. The problem is that, ordinarily, any other answer than 16 is "not correct," and the divergent thinker may then run a higher risk of making mistakes or looking foolish. But there are two aspects to consider in this scenario:

1) Most important problems in real life do not have one correct answer. There is no one correct way to design a house or sell more widgets or write an interesting novel.

2) Studies indicate that willingness to take cognitive risks is a particularly salient trait of highly creative individuals.

A young man once went hiking in the woods. Unfortunately, he stumbled and began to fall down a precipice. On the way to his sure death, however, he was able to grab the branch of a tree that was growing from the side of the mountain. As he hung there in midair, unable to move, and feeling his fingers slowly loosening their grasp, he looked up to the heavens and said, "Please, won't somebody help me?" He heard a deep voice from above say, "Yes, son, what is the trouble?" He replied, "Please help, I'll do anything." The deep voice replied, "Let go of the tree." The young man looked down—it was quite a distance to the bottom. He then looked up and said, "Is there anyone else up there?" When we are trying to come up with a creative solution, we often need to let go of what seem to be safe habits and trite solutions. But, like that young man, we are afraid to truly let go of our fears and habits.

Judy Collins is a well-known folk singer who has entertained large audiences with her golden voice and guitar accompaniment. As a youngster and teenager, she studied classical piano, beginning at about age three. She was quite good, but then heard a folk song over the radio ("Barbara Allen," sung by Jo Stafford) and switched from classical to folk music. She tells us that, when she switched, she felt "ecstasy," and that her life became filled with creativity.

Change in Perception

Have you ever had an experience like this? You lose the little screw that holds the frame of your glasses together. You need your glasses to drive to the optician to get them fixed, so you need a temporary repair. You try Scotch tape, but it's too flimsy. You consider duct tape, but it's too bulky. You are now desperate, so you try a wad of chewing gum, but it doesn't stay put. You happen to see a paper clip on the desk and realize it can be used as a temporary pin in place of the lost screw. The solution basically involved seeing everyday objects (chewing gum and the paper clip) in a different light—perceiving that a paper clip can be used as a pin.

Creative solutions often involve changes in perception—seeing an everyday object in a different light, perceiving the potential of an idea that at first was rejected, seeing a new relationship, and so on. Such alterations in perception can occur "spontaneously," or can be induced by changes in our bodies, such as fatigue, the fever that accompanies an illness, falling asleep, feeling drowsy, strong emotions, or mind-altering substances ranging from alcohol to peyote. Unfortunately, there are many concomitant problems associated with inducing changes in perception.

Obviously, we shouldn't go out and expose ourselves to serious illnesses just to experience the feverish bouts that might accompany that illness. Similarly, illegal drugs, while they may alter our perception, also affect our ability to actually create. Artists who ingested such mind-altering substances thought they were being highly creative, but in fact produced drawings that were not creative at all.

> Kekule, a chemist-researcher, had been working on the chemical structure of benzene, but unsuccessfully. He dozed by a fireplace and began to see, in his mind's eye, atoms bouncing and dancing before him, and being transformed into snakes. He noticed that one of the snakes had chomped onto its own tail forming a whirling circle. Kekule woke up from his reverie and realized that this was the solution he had been searching for—the structure of benzene can be expressed in chemical terms as a ring.

Isabel Allende, the well-known novelist and niece of Salvadore Allende, former president of Chile, says that when she sees a gadget like a blender she imagines how she can use it for something else. How often do we look at a blender and only see a blender?

Think of the daily newspaper. What are some of the different ways you could use a newspaper (e.g., to wrap a present, to send a ransom note, to start a fire, etc.)? How about a pencil? Can a pencil be used for something other than writing? What about a dead fish? A fork? A 3 x 5 index card?

Tolerance for Ambiguity

One aspect of creative persons studied by psychologists is that creative persons tend to have a high tolerance for ambiguity. Most of us prefer to have the world in black and white terms, to know when a meeting is supposed to start, to have a diagnostic label for our ailments, to at least know the name and occupation of people we meet socially. In most creative undertakings, we don't have the full picture; we don't have all the rules that can guide our behavior (think how uncreative painting by the numbers is). In many creative endeavors, we might not know what the end result will be, and sometimes we don't even know what the initial challenge is. I may want to express the feeling of love in a painting, but it may turn out that the feeling is lust, and the painting I tentatively envisioned of a well-rounded woman in the style of Reubens may eventuate in an abstract painting closer to Picasso's style.

Personality

People who are highly creative tend to have certain personality traits. Keep in mind that creative people come in all sizes and shapes, and what may be typical may not necessarily describe a lot of creative people. Human nature is just too complex to be defined by a number of categories. Nevertheless, here are some of the many characteristics that describe highly creative persons:

1. They are achievement oriented. Their tenacity and persistence will lead them to the goals they seek.
2. They are curious and intellectually alive. Like a child who asks, "Why? Why? Why?", they have an insatiable curiosity about the world.
3. They are less concerned with everyday conventionality, with the niceties of everyday social transactions. They do not always appear to be unconventional. Wearing sandals and a ponytail are not necessarily the trappings of a creative person.
4. They have a wide range of interests and are knowledgeable in many areas.

5. They view the world from an aesthetic rather than a judgmental point of view, and are more concerned with beauty and ugliness than with goodness and badness.
6. They are open to their inner emotional life. They are in touch with their feelings, with their emotional pain and their joys.
7. They tend to be introverted, particularly in not actively seeking interpersonal relationships and not valuing social interactions.
8. They are aware of their creativity and inventiveness.
9. They have a substantial degree of empathy and intuitiveness. When our two daughters were four and six years old, at the dinner table the older picked up her fork, looked through it at her younger sister and said, "You look like you're in prison." The younger sister in turn picked up her fork, looked at her older sister and said, "Well, you look like you're in prison looking through a fork!" What a marvelous creative interaction, and, for a four-year-old, what a sense of empathy. If I may be permitted a bit of parental boasting, both daughters have grown into wonderful, highly creative adults.
10. They have a greater impact on others.

It's Either Black or White (Not!)

My high school and college years were spent in small, private institutions. When it came to discipline and logic, I feel that I obtained an excellent education. But when it came to creativity, to openness to ideas, tolerance of ambiguity, and imagination, the majority of my instructors fell sadly on their faces. When I arrived in graduate school, surrounded by fellow classmates who were truly brilliant, taught by faculty members who were at the cutting edge of their field, I realized how I had been short-changed. My first year in graduate school was a near disaster, primarily because I had not been given the education I needed, both in convergent knowledge and divergent thinking. Perhaps that is why I became so interested in creativity, as well as other psychological topics.

If you, too, were brought up to think in black and white terms, begin to realize now that most of life is made up of truly gray areas, and that to be creative means to be open to a variety of ideas and solutions. If you're not convinced, just read the letters to the editor in any newspaper or magazine. You will find a wide variety of views on a specific topic, and most of these views will diverge from yours; surely, not everyone else is wrong while you are right!

The Qwerty Approach

Just about everyone recognizes the letters "QWERTY" as the first row of letters on a typewriter or computer keyboard. The sequence of these letters goes back to the 1800's, when the typewriter was invented. One of the early problems was that, as typists became proficient, the typewriter keys would stick together when rapidly hit. The challenge here, then, was to slow down the typist—this was done by creating a keyboard layout that was not very efficient, with some of the alphabet letters that occur frequently in the English language being placed where they would be hit by "weaker" fingers. As typewriters improved (and, of course, with computer keyboards), sticking keys were no longer a major problem, but the QWERTY keyboard has stayed with us.

The point here is that life is filled with rules and procedures that probably made sense at some point and are still followed, though the reasons for them are now obsolete. "We've been doing that for years, and we will continue doing it this way" has become a golden rule for many businesses and individuals.

Recently, we purchased an expensive bedroom set from a well-known furniture company. Within a few months, the side railing broke. When I contacted the customer service rep and suggested that they could FedEx the replacement railing, his reply was "We don't do FedEx." I told him there was a local branch of his company in Tucson, and that they had the side railing in stock; again his reply was that this was not possible. I had to wait for over a month to get the side railing replaced. The company lost the opportunity to sell me additional furniture and to create customer goodwill, simply because one of their employees (and the manager, as well) could not think in a flexible manner.

In trying to reach a creative solution, then, one of the first things to do is challenge the rules—ask whether we need to do it this way. Are we making assumptions that need not be made?

At most colleges and universities, most classes are 3-credit classes, which means that the class meets three times a week for a 50-minute period. I always thought this was not an efficient use of time but, try as I might to change this, I was unsuccessful. For some classes I taught, meeting once a week for three hours seemed more efficient. For other classes, twice a week for 90 minutes seemed a better use of time. I had some department heads tell me, "We've always scheduled classes three times a week" or "Students cannot sit still for three hours." The registrar (the office that, among other things, schedules classes) was strongly opposed to any such changes, claiming at first it would be chaotic, and then that it would go against "tried and true" procedures. I managed to bypass these naysayers, and did teach a seminar on creativity that met once a week for three hours in an off-campus studio (officially, the class met three times a week in a sterile classroom). The course was a great success, and some of the students still reminisce about what a great experience it was. In fact, the college environment is full of rules and regulations that do nothing but stifle learning and inhibit creativity, yet the whole governance of a college is precisely designed like the QWERTY keyboard—to have things run smoothly by slowing down productivity!

Creativity and Routine

Think about how you get dressed in the morning. Most likely, it is a highly "routinized" procedure. If you wear slacks or pants, chances are that you typically put the same leg in first. If you brush your teeth, you most likely start in the same place in your mouth, day after day. You probably have a favorite brand of coffee, and you keep your cutlery in the same drawer. Obviously, such routine is in large part necessary. You don't want to spend half an hour each morning searching for a coffee spoon, or reassessing how much sugar and milk in your coffee tastes best to you. At the same time, such routines are like the blinders that the now defunct milk delivery horses wore. They didn't allow the horse to be distracted, but simply to focus on the path ahead. Much of creativity involves straying from the well-traveled path, really looking at what we "see" everyday (but don't notice), and perceiving the world differently. I often suggested to my college students to try altering their routine—to start brushing the left side of their mouth rather than the right side. The feedback was typically a shaking of the head (as if to say "another nutty professor"), or a forgetting to try (habits are very strong), or a report that they tried once, but then reverted to their more typical pattern of behavior.

I don't know if this is a myth or not, but it is said that the US Army continued to make and issue uniforms that had a pocket for a watch fully twenty-five years after pocket watches had been replaced by wristwatches.

Focusing on the Right Answer

The more educated you are, the more likely you are to be an expert at coming up with the right answer—at convergent thinking. Much of what is education consists of learning what the right answer is, beginning with the alphabet (what comes after c?) to college level physics (how do you compute the number of watts required in a particular circumstance?). Such "right" knowledge is, of course, required in a lot of human activities. The beauty of creativity is that it transcends the "right" answer. If you have a $100 budget with which to decorate your room, there is no one right answer, but a multitude of possible answers—some, to be sure, not able to be implemented or representing "bad" ideas (e.g., buying $100 worth of cockroaches to cluster on the walls).

Quite often, when we are faced with a challenge, there are a number of ways to solve that challenge. One of my favorite ways to illustrate that point is with the following question: Is 1,000,008 perfectly divisible by 9 (i.e., no remainder)? One way to solve this problem is to use a calculator and divide 1,000,008 by 9 to see that, yes, it is perfectly divisible by 9 with no remainder. Another way is to remember a rule that most of us learned in school: add the individual digits of the number and if they add up to 9 (in this case 1+8) then the number is perfectly divisible by 9 (e.g., 1323, 4374, and 77058 are all perfectly divisible by 9—we don't need a calculator). Still a third way to solve this problem is to realize that 1,000,008 represents the sum of 999,999 + 9, and so, of course, the number is perfectly divisible by 9. We don't need a calculator, and we don't need a rule—all we need is the insight! This solution has a simplicity and elegance to it, much like most creative solutions. If you solved this little problem by the third way, you will have most likely noticed that your solution was practically instantaneous and quite vivid—perhaps you even saw the 999,999 and 9 in your mind's eye. If you didn't use the third approach, don't feel bad—most people don't. The point is to keep an open mind. In many cases, there is more than one "right" answer!

Same Becomes Different

Another way of looking at creativity is that the process of creativity involves looking at an everyday object in a different and unusual way. I am sure you have seen articles in your local paper or some magazine about a sculptor who gets pieces of scrap metal, like seats from an old tractor and discarded plumbing, and welds them together into a sculpture of an animal or a person.

There are several ways to foster this type of creativity. One is to select a common object (for example, a pencil) and imagine how else that pencil could be used: as a dart in a barroom game, as a chopstick, to plug holes in the wall, or as a swing for a parakeet. A very talented architect I know designed, as a student, a chair made totally of pencils.

Another way is to take that same object and ask, "What if?" What if we made pencils square rather than round? What if both ends were pointed? What if the pencil contained a lotion that made your hands stronger? What if we impregnated the wood with fluoride? What if pencils were three feet long? What if pencils were encased in rubber housings, so they could be bounced like balls? What if pencils were made of plastic instead of wood?

Creativity and Knowledge

Creativity flourishes in an environment of knowledge, but often it is disparate knowledge that makes the difference. Let me explain. It would be difficult, for example, for a musician to be a creative composer (as opposed to a technical virtuoso) without having a fundamental knowledge of music notation, harmony, fingering, etc. Similarly, an inventor trying to design a different type of vacuum cleaner needs to have some knowledge about electricity, rotary brushes, the force of compressed air, etc. Such knowledge can be informal, intuitive, or obtained through practical experience rather than formal training, but it needs to be there.

But, often, what distinguishes a technical expert from a truly creative person is that the creative individual also possesses a lot of knowledge about a lot of things. Often, the knowledge appears to be of the "trivia" kind, but, typically, such a wide range of knowledge reflects a high degree of curiosity and alertness to the world. There is an old analogy I like to use, even though it is a bit outdated. Remember the old library card catalogs? They were wonderful pieces of furniture with lots of little drawers containing 3 x 5 cards that listed information about each book. The human brain is something like that catalog. We file facts and bits of information in different drawers. To be creative requires more drawers (because we have more facts), as well as the capacity to select cards from different drawers—cards that ordinarily do not belong together, but, when joined, offer a creative solution.

Robert J. Lang is a very bright and respected research scientist, the author of more than eighty technical papers and the holder of forty-six patents. In 2001, he left his job with a California fiber optics company in order to pursue his true passion full time: origami. Origami, as you probably know, involves shaping sheets of paper into three-dimensional objects, using no cutting and no glue. If your initial reaction is "What a waste of time," you should know that origami folding techniques have a wide range of electrical, optical, and medical applications. In fact, Lang has written some very sophisticated computer programs that guide such folding in these applications.

Lang is considered a world expert in origami folding, a field that has always been dominated by the Japanese. His interest in origami started at age six, when he was given an origami book by a teacher to keep him entertained in math class. Little Robert was a math whiz, and by the time he was in his early teens he was designing his own origami patterns. He kept up with his passion while studying electrical engineering at Caltech, earning a master's degree at Stanford, and a doctorate in applied physics at Caltech. (Orlean, 2007)

Expertise

Although it could be possible for a professional chef to design a new electronic gizmo to guide smart bombs, it would be highly unlikely. To be creative in any one field most likely requires a great deal of expertise in that field. Most creative painters, for example, also know a great deal about the mechanics of painting, about the composition of brushes, the way colors interact with light, about perspective and curves, and so on. Knowledge is not only power, it is also, in most cases, a prerequisite to creativity. A master gardener knows not only about plants, but about soils, drainage, fertilizers, and photosynthesis.

The problem with expertise, with knowledge, is that it can become a habit; it can blind us to innovation. As experts, we believe we have the right answer; we "know" that nothing else will work as well, and we look with condescension at neophytes who have the temerity to suggest an alternate approach.

Edwin Land, the inventor of the Polaroid camera, came to his invention because his three-year-old daughter asked him why she could not see a photograph immediately

> after it was taken. Had the daughter been an "expert" in photography and knowledgeable about the chemical process involved, she would have never asked such a "ridiculous" question.

EVALUATION

Eventually, creative insights need to be verified, to be evaluated. The painter needs to look at her paintings with a critical eye, and the inventor at her inventions with cold logic. Be careful, however, of evaluation. Often, when a person comes to this step, there are many others ready to shoot the idea down, to criticize it, to point out all the faults and potential problems. One way to minimize this evaluative set is to look at the proposed solution being evaluated and to first list all the positive aspects of that solution, all the strengths and promises. Then list the negative aspects or concerns why the proposed solution will not work. List these not as statements of fact (Our competition will laugh), but as a question (Will our competition laugh?). Listing an objection as a question will almost automatically require an answer (Yes, they will laugh, but so what? No, they won't laugh. No, they will want to copy our design. No, they will wonder why they didn't think of it. Yes, they will laugh, and so will we—all the way to the bank!).

Quite often, we use adjectives to evaluate solutions: "That's a dumb idea," "The results will be too slow," "That painting is pretty ugly." Psychologists, in their infinite wisdom, have concluded that, when we use adjectives to evaluate something, we are most likely to evaluate our target along three dimensions: good vs. bad (Is this a good idea?), strong vs. weak (Is this a powerful advertisement?), and fast vs. slow (How soon can we implement this?). There are, of course, many more dimensions we could and do use. In rating a potentially creative solution, we could evaluate the solution according to:

1. How cheap or expensive it might be to implement.
2. How familiar the solution might be.
3. How old or new the idea is (is it a variation on a common solution or something really new?).
4. How earth-shaking it is (is this a new drug that will save lives or a new flavor of bubble-gum?).
5. How logical the solution appears to the consumer.
6. How general the solution is (can it be applied to a whole range of similar problems or is it very specific?)

These are fairly logical questions, but we can also be creative in our evaluation. For example, we could evaluate our potentially creative solution along the dimensions of:

Tall-short	Permanent-transitional
Angular-circular	Organized-disorganized
Dirty-clean	Exciting-boring
Pretty-homely	Effervescent-flat

Ray Bradbury is probably best known for his novel, *Dandelion Wine*, and his science fiction work, *The Martian Chronicles*. He is a prolific writer who has written screenplays, operas, novels, and stage plays.

What words of advice does Ray Bradbury give to neophyte writers? "There is no substitute for hard work," and if you want to write, you must do it every day. Furthermore, you should pursue anything you have a passion for. Ray Bradbury writes at least a thousand words every day. He writes whatever comes to his mind, and then goes back later to judge critically. He finds his inspiration and ideas in the poetry of others.

> Another writer, J. G. Ballard (*The Day of Creation*, *Empire of the Sun*) writes at least 800 words every day.

AGE AND CREATIVITY

Don't use age as an excuse that you can no longer produce creative ideas, that creativity is for the young, not for the "senior citizen."

Did you know that Giuseppe Verdi was still composing operas in his seventies and eighties?

Did you know that Frank Lloyd Wright designed the Guggenheim Museum in New York City when he was ninety-one?

Did you know that Dr. Seuss continued writing his zany and beloved books well into his eighties?

The Marshall Plan, a blueprint for the reconstruction of Europe after the Second World War, was named for George C. Marshall, who, at age sixty-seven, became Secretary of State. He was awarded the Nobel Peace Prize at the age of seventy-three.

Elizabeth Garrett Anderson, the first woman to become a physician in England, was, at age seventy-two, also the first woman to be elected a mayor in England.

Carl Jung, the well-known psychiatrist, was eighty-six when he completed his autobiography.

No doubt you have heard of Granny Smith apples, a very popular item in grocery stores. They are the result of experiments conducted by Maria Ann Smith of Australia, who was in her sixties at the time.

One of the best-known figures in modern dance was Martha Graham. She choreographed her last work ("Maple Leaf Rag") when she was ninety-six! (Cohen, 2000)

There are many more examples; creativity does not know age limits. No matter how young or old you are, don't use age as an excuse not to practice your creative potential.

Too Few or Too Many Ideas

Some people have difficulty generating ideas. Faced with a problem that requires creative solutions, they freeze up, or believe they are not creative and, therefore, any ideas they might generate simply cannot be worth anything. If that is your problem, you should realize that creativity is like intelligence or muscle strength. Even the dumbest person can solve some challenges, and even the weakest person can lift some object. The point here is to build up that muscle strength to its fullest potential, and many of the exercises in this book will hopefully do that for your creativity.

Other people suffer from the opposite problem—they have too many ideas, and the very flood of ideas paralyzes them. The solution here is to make your ideas work *for* you, rather than against you. Write them down. Put them in a list according to "promise" (which ideas might be more fruitful, or easier to implement, or more personally challenging). Select five ideas for further consideration (if you have to, toss a coin to decide which five).

> I love music and have a CD collection of about 1000 titles. Sometimes, it can be overwhelming to try and select two or three CDs to play. I want to hear some music, but too many choices come to mind. So I ask myself, "What mood am I in?" Do I want something classical that will make my blood rush—perhaps an overture by Rossini? Or do I want something happy and with a good beat, like a Greek song by Nana Mouskouri? Do I want to hear someone like Luciano Pavarotti singing Sicilian songs or operatic arias that might remind me of my ethnic roots? Or perhaps a Mariachi medley that is consonant with my living in the Southwest? Or perhaps the wonderful

accordion sound of Flaco Jimenez, as he bemoans the fact that there is no beer in heaven? If I answer "yes" to most questions, then I simply put the chosen CD's on the stereo and let them play. If I need to, I do it randomly. If necessary, I reach on the shelves semi-blindly and select by the method of "serendipity" (with my eyes closed!). The point is that, even with too many ideas, you can still make a selection, whether guided or random.

The topics above have been listed and discussed in general terms. Occasionally, I asked a few specific questions for you to consider, but the intent was to provide some general parameters. It's like learning to drive. Before you can sit behind the wheel and turn on the ignition, a person needs to have some appreciation that driving is not a right, that you need to be careful and courteous, that there are certain issues of personal and legal responsibility, and so on. The same principle applies to creativity. Now we are ready to look at some more specific ideas.

Chapter 3

How To Enhance Your Creativity

Dreams

Dreams are the topic of hundreds of books ranging from academic tomes that will put you to sleep in a few minutes to books filled with pure nonsense about the nature and meaning of dreams. Even among psychologists who study dreaming, there is great disagreement as to the nature and purpose of dreaming, with some psychologists believing that dreams reflect unconscious wishes and fantasies, while others believe dreams are mental garbage, and that dreaming represents a nightly cleaning process in which the brain engages.

For the purposes of creativity, however, the evidence very clearly supports the view that dreams can be helpful in solving problems and, because dreams involve visual thinking (we dream in images rather than words), they can be particularly useful in solving problems that require a visual, rather than a verbal, approach. Dreams also represent an altered state of awareness that can allow us to look at a problem from a somewhat different perspective. With some minor exceptions, dreams are unique. Not only are my dreams quite different from yours, but, even with the same person, each dream is usually different. Quite often, dreams involve the creation of a new pattern. I might dream of Uncle Butch in the body of a voluptuous woman with the voice of a child, but I recognize him because he is smoking his usual smelly cigar!

A friend once gave me, as a gift, a book of puzzles taken, I believe, from a magazine called *Scientific American*. Prior to bedtime, I read one of the simpler puzzles. It was about three men who have different occupations. A number of hints were given (e.g., John is married to the cousin of the plumber) by which the reader could solve the puzzle. I struggled with it with no success, and fell asleep quite frustrated. I then had a very vivid dream. Three toy soldiers were marching around very stiffly, bumping into each other, falling down and getting up. This went on for what seemed like a long while, with the three soldiers, little by little, moving into the background towards three guard huts, such as one might find outside a European palace. In my dream, I followed the three soldiers until each had entered a guard hut, and I noticed that each hut had a sign on it. The first sign said "John Plumber," the second said "Carl Electrician," and the third said "Paul Mechanic." I woke up and checked the answer in the back of the puzzle book. Sure enough, my dream had provided me with a colorful and correct solution to the problem.

Here's another example from my personal experience: Years ago, I was teaching a graduate seminar on dreams, and I asked each student to prepare a research proposal for a new study they could reasonably carry out on the topic of dreams. One young lady proposed a study involving dreams and a personality dimension. She had done a good job in her proposal, but the only problem was that a study such as she proposed had already been carried out, and somewhere I had read about it. When I told her this, she said she had done very thorough research of the literature and had not come across such a study. I did not doubt her, and I could not provide her with a reference to the study I was thinking of. I did a thorough search also and simply could not find the phantom study (this was in the days before computers). That evening, I had the following dream: I was standing next to this student, berating her for her sloppy work, and I proceeded to hit her over the head with a heavy, black book. The dream was rather bizarre, particularly since I am a fairly peaceful type of person, not given to physical violence. In my dream, I realized that the book I hit her with looked exactly like a doctoral dissertation (in our university library, they are all bound in black). I told myself, in my dream, to look at the book, and noticed that the spine contained the letters "UNC 1968." I woke up and wrote down that information. In the morning, I called the research librarian at the University of North Carolina and explained that I was looking for a doctoral dissertation done there in 1968 on the topic of dreams and personality (I did not tell her about my dream!). She called back later and, indeed, told me there was such a dissertation, and she would send it to me on interlibrary loan. Incidentally, this type of dream, where you know you are dreaming while you are dreaming, is called a lucid dream (see page 78).

There are literally hundreds of recorded examples of dreams that resulted in some significant problem solution, a painting, a poem, or an invention. For example, the well-known story of *Dr. Jekyll and Mr. Hyde* by Robert Louis Stevenson was the result of a dream in which Stevenson eluded some pursuers by drinking a potion that changed his appearance. The epic poem, "Kubla Khan," by Samuel Taylor Coleridge was also the result of dreams. I've mentioned the famous chemist, August Kekule von Stradonitz (better known as Kekule), who discovered the chemical formula of the benzene ring by "dreaming" of a snake with its tail in its mouth. Niels Bohr, the famous physicist, developed a model of the atom based on a dream he had of the solar system. Elias Howe, the inventor of the sewing machine, attributed his success to a dream that allowed him to solve a mechanical problem he had been wrestling with. Dreams were apparently the stimuli for invasions of Spain and of Italy. In the Moorish invasion of Spain, Tarq, the leader of the Moors, dreamt of Mohammed and his army, and so invaded the Spanish province of Andalucia. Hannibal invaded Italy after a dream of a giant serpent moving along and destroying everything in its path. Richard Wagner, the German composer, based the major motif of his epic opera, "The Ring of the Nibelung," on a "dream" he experienced as he was falling asleep. He imagined that he was immersed in rapidly flowing water, and perceived the rushing sound as a musical sound in the key of E flat major! We should at the same time, view such incidents with a healthy dose of skepticism. For example, Niels Bohr, some fifty years later, was asked directly about his dream of the planets spinning around the sun; he not only denied having such a dream, but also commented that his dreams had never helped him in any practical way!

One of the problems with dreams is that they are very "fragile" as memories; unless we make an effort to capture them, they are easily gone. How do we capture them? With dreams, intention is nine-tenths of the law. If you intend to remember your dreams, that will help. Secondly, have something available on which to write down your dreams in the middle of the night. As you probably know, sleep is cyclical. We fall asleep and fall into deeper and deeper sleep. Then we "resurface" into lighter sleep. We do this several times a night. We dream when we are in the lighter stages of sleep, almost awake. These cycles have another interesting property. As the night progresses, the time spent in dreaming gets longer, and the dreams we do remember are typically from our early morning cycles, rather than when we first go to sleep, or from the middle of the night. Gore Vidal, the novelist and screenwriter, stated that he writes shortly after waking up because then he is closest to the dream world.

If you can, don't wake up with an alarm clock—it is too disruptive of dream memories. Open your eyes and stay as you are for a couple of minutes. If you remember a dream, write it down.

The May 2004 issue of *Popular Science* reports on Jake Lyall, who built a monowheel: a motorized, one-wheel vehicle. Visualize a very large wheel with a Honda scooter engine on the inside of the wheel and a spring-mounted seat for the driver on the outside of the wheel. One-wheeled vehicles, or monowheels, have existed since the 1800's. Most of them look like a giant squirrel cage, with the driver sitting inside the cage and pedaling for all he's worth.

What is interesting here is that Mr. Lyall has never worked for a garage and has never studied engineering. He is a part-time computer programmer and a Renaissance Fair jouster. He also claims that the idea for his invention came to him in a dream (you can see his invention, as well as pictures and descriptions of earlier monowheels, at: www.theriotwheel.com).

Lucid Dreams

We sometimes realize that we are dreaming while we are dreaming, rather than after we wake up. This type of dream has been labeled a lucid dream, and is of particular interest to dream researchers.

The history of dreams is a long and fascinating one. You are probably familiar with several dreams reported in the Bible that typically represented messages from God. You might have read accounts of how dreams guided primitive societies, or how dreams were seen as the work of the Devil in the Middle Ages. Most likely, you are familiar with some of the writings of Sigmund Freud, who perceived dreams as the doorway to the unconscious.

The actual scientific study of dreams, however, only began in 1953, when a graduate student by the name of Eugene Aserinsky, working in the sleep laboratory of Professor Nathaniel Kleitman, began studying the eye movements of infants during sleep. These eye movements followed a fairly regular pattern and could be easily observed through the almost transparent eyelids that infants have. Aserinsky wondered if the eye movements indicated that the infants were "watching" their dreams, and so proceeded to study this phenomenon in adults who could, in fact, report with words what was going on. By recording the eye movements electrically, Aserinsky and Kleitman discovered a regular pattern of sleep episodes of rapid eye movement (REM); when they woke their subjects during these periods, the subjects reported quite vivid dreams, but when awakened outside these periods, subjects reported few or no dreams. Another interesting finding was that these periods of rapid eye movement and dreaming occurred when the subject was in light sleep, rather than deep sleep. This basic research was the foundation of the scientific study of dreams, uniting psychological and physiological viewpoints.

What are dreams? Unfortunately, we still do not have an answer that most scientists would endorse. Some hold on to the Freudian view. Others believe that dreams actually consist of individual, random images that our sleeping brain "explains" by weaving them into a story. Other scientists (like Nobel winner Francis Crick) believe that dreams are basically garbage generated by our brain; just as we have trash around our house that we clean out regularly, we have "trash" in our psychological-physiological functioning that the brain cleans out nightly. For our purposes, we can think of dreams as thinking that occurs at night. It is primarily visual thinking (i.e., we think in pictures and symbols, rather than words), and that is why dreaming is so relevant to creativity: much of creativity requires visual thinking.

How Can You Access Your Dreams?

By and large, our culture does not value dreams. Although we might share with friends and family an "interesting" dream we have had, the focus is typically on how bizarre and entertaining (or scary) dreams can be, rather than any usefulness they might have. Dreams are truly "garbage" as far as our attitudes go, and so we don't really pay attention to them. Imagine if garbage were truly precious—you would pay great attention to it. Think of a time when you might have lost a piece of jewelry in the trash, and how carefully you poked and prodded that trash. Similarly, if we, as a society, believed that dreams could be useful as far as creativity is concerned, we would most likely pay close attention to them. Please note that, as a scientist, I do not believe there is evidence to support the notion that dreams predict the future, or that they are long-distance messages from either above or below. As a clinical psychologist, I also believe dreams have limited value as a psychotherapeutic technique, and that there are better ways to help patients than through dream analysis. But, as thinking that occurs at night, I believe dreams can be very useful as a way of generating creative ideas.

To facilitate access to your dreams, you must first pay attention to them. You must be convinced that your dreams can be an interesting and potentially useful source of material for creative use. Whatever you do, however, don't pay attention to the large number of "dream manuals" that are available, the ones that tell you that, if you dream about the loss of a tooth, someone in your family is going to die, and if you dream of the mail-carrier, you will receive good news within the next three days. For the most part, those books are filled with nonsense.

Another step that can be helpful, but is not necessary, is to develop a sensitivity and awareness of your inner psychological life. Try to tune in to your inner moods, your motivation, your likes and dislikes, your psychological strengths, and your weak spots. Obviously, this can't be done overnight, and I'm not suggesting you enter psychotherapy! Learning to meditate can be useful in this endeavor, but I would not recommend studying meditation within a religious context, particularly one that presents meditation as the solution to all of life's problems.

The easiest step to implement is to tell yourself that you *will* pay attention to your dreams. Therefore, you will have a pad and pencil at your nightstand, ready to record your dreams the minute you awaken from them. Notice that dreams are part of what is called short-term memory. If you have ever looked in the phone book for a number, dialed it, and a minute later realize that you don't remember it—that's short term memory. Therefore, when you dream and wake up, don't get up immediately. Lie quietly and let your mind "capture" that dream in a more permanent form before you write it down. If you can awaken without an alarm clock or without a boisterous pet dog licking your face, do so.

A useful way of thinking about a dream is to realize it is a story that you, the dreamer, have created. Therefore, you hold the meaning (or, more accurately, the meanings) of the dream.

In the context of creativity, the meaning may not be so important—what is important are the possible insights and solutions related to the creative problem you are facing.

Once you begin to remember your dreams in a more or less reliable manner, then you can start telling yourself, before you fall asleep, that "tonight I will dream about x, y, or z"—whatever the creative challenge is that you are facing. Some people can make this work, and many others cannot. If it's important to you, don't give up.

Finally, remember that, quite often, dreams can have a disturbing side to them. It is not unusual to find dreams not only "interesting," but also unpleasant, and sometimes downright disturbing. In actual surveys of dream content, negative emotions like anger and fear tend to occur twice as often as positive emotions like happiness. There are some people who are psychologically fragile and do not need the added stress of remembering unpleasant dreams.

> Giuseppe Tartini was an Italian violinist and composer who lived in the 1700's. He is best remembered for a solo violin sonata called "Devil's Trill Sonata," a very difficult piece to play because it is technically demanding. There are a number of legends surrounding this piece. One is that Tartini had six fingers on his left hand, and thus could play this composition more easily! Another legend was that Tartini dreamt one night that he gave his violin to the Devil, whereupon the Devil played a most beautiful composition. When Tartini woke up, he tried to recapture the piece, and this "Devil's Trill Sonata" became his best work, even though what he wrote was inferior to the Devil's performance in his dream.

THE "OTHER" TYPE OF DREAM

There are not only night dreams, but also the "dreams" we all have, buried somewhere deep down, of being a success, or starting our own business, or being swept off our feet by a knight in shining armor. This is another meaning of the word "dream"—the hopes and wishes we have. For most of us, these dreams seem unattainable, simply because we focus on the end result (being rich), rather than on the steps we need to take to achieve that end result. To someone who wants to diet, losing 25 or 50 pounds seems unattainable, and so the person dreams of being svelte, but takes no steps towards that goal. But just about anyone can lose one pound. It might take a week or more, but it is doable. So go ahead and do it, and then repeat it, and repeat it, and repeat it! If you have a dream, be creative in order to achieve it. Brainstorm, or use some of the other techniques in this book to come up with ideas that you can implement to reach your goal.

PRINCIPLES OF ASSOCIATION

Psychologists and philosophers speak of three basic principles of association:

1. CONTIGUITY: when two items occur near each other. For example, when I think of Bill, I think of the pipe he smokes. Bill and pipe are associated in my mind by virtue of their proximity or contiguity.

2. SIMILARITY: the two items share some properties in common. For example, a blowfish might remind me of a beach ball, simply because both have a spherical shape.

3. CONTRAST: the two items have some characteristics in opposition to each other. For example, a lion might bring to mind a church mouse. These two differ in size (large vs. small), in temperament (ferocious vs. timid), and so on.

Most of us can easily play the "game" of association. If I say the word "black," you would probably reply with "white." If I say "mother," you might say "father," and so on. A lot of what we learn in life is through association. Most drivers have learned that a traffic light turning red means to put on the brake (a few drivers have learned to associate it with pressing down on the accelerator). To be creative means we have a greater network of associations, and that these associations are more "remote" from each other. A creative driver will be as likely to stop at a red light as a less creative driver, but the creative driver may wonder why a red light that means "stop" is also a symbol for an unsavory district, or why red is a symbol for communism, or why communism and prostitution have this symbol in common.

Creativity As Association

One way to think about creativity is to see innovative thinking as the result of two disparate ideas that ordinarily do not belong together nevertheless coming together. Here are some examples:

Toothpaste + cleaning jewelry results in a paste for cleaning jewelry.

Wheels + chair results in an office chair.

Flower + lion results in a poetic metaphor.

Wine press + coin punch results in the printing press.

How can we get disparate ideas to come together for a potentially creative solution? Here are some methods:

1. The dictionary is a gold mine of disparate ideas that are listed alphabetically. Open the dictionary at random in two separate places and write down two words from separate locations. For example, take the two words, "hat" and "naval." Quite readily, these two words bring up the

image of graduating West Point or Annapolis cadets joyously tossing their hats into the air. Immediately, a series of questions comes to mind. How did this tradition originate? Are the hats retrieved? Is there a company that retrieves them? (Perhaps we need a service to retrieve lost or misplaced items?) How much damage is done to the hats? (Perhaps the hats should be made of a stronger material?) Should we design a hat that, like a boomerang, comes back to its owner? If you were a freelance writer, the joining of these two words could provide you with a great topic for a magazine article. If you're looking to be self-employed, this might provide the impetus for a business.

When I was in high school and took an American history course, the instructor told us to write a term paper on any topic we chose within the confines of the course. The great majority of us chose pretty standard topics—perhaps a famous historical figure like Abraham Lincoln, or a battle from the Civil War, and so on. One of my classmates produced an issue of *TV Guide* as it might have existed at the time of George Washington. It was so well done and creative that the student was asked to present his paper to the entire class. When asked how he came up with the topic, he indicated he had been trying to think of a term paper topic for a couple of weeks, with no success. Finally, the day before he was to hand in his topic, he looked at a *TV Guide*, thought of George Washington, and voila!

2. Quite often, you already have the first word or idea, because you are working on a problem. For example, Velcro

was invented by George de Mestral, who noticed, after a walk in the woods, that cockleburs held on tenaciously to his clothes. He had probably been thinking about different ways in which articles of clothing could be closed, but certainly the idea of "cockleburs" had not occurred to him before his walk. So sometimes all that is needed is exposure to an unrelated idea—whether it's through a walk in the woods, a ride on a train, looking at a book of photographs, or randomly flipping the pages of a dictionary.

3. I love 3 x 5 cards, and I think they are an indispensable tool in the area of creativity. Let's say that you work in advertising, specifically in creating new packages for food and sundry products. Did you ever notice that many of these products come in highly distinguishable packages? For example, anchovies come in small rectangular tins that are very difficult and messy to open. Milk comes in cartons or bottles. Vegetables come in round cans. Bread is in plastic or paper bags, and so on.

   Now take two stacks of 3 x 5 cards. On one stack, write a product's name on each card (e.g., olive oil, toothpaste, crackers). On the other stack, write or draw a type of package (e.g., round can, flat box, cylinder, etc.). Now select at random a card from one stack and one from the other stack—for example, olive oil and paper bag. Consider these two ideas together. Your first impulse might be to dismiss this as crazy. After all, olive oil packaged in a paper bag just would not work. But wait. Aren't there fruit juices and milk packaged in "paper bags"? Of course, even though they are sturdy and waxed, they are paper bags nevertheless. Continue playing with the two ideas. Perhaps you'll think of a traditional metal can for the olive oil, but one covered by a colorful paper bag, perhaps less expensive to print than the current metal cans. Or perhaps you'll wonder whether olive oil, like some wines, can be packaged in a plastic-lined box. Perhaps the two ideas will lead you to wonder whether square oil cans can hold paper bags, or whether you can use the imagery (visualize a paper bag soaked and dripping in olive oil) in a poem or story you might write.

You might find that the notion of paper bag leads to the idea of purse (a cloth bag), and the concept of olive oil brings to mind your favorite Italian restaurant—and these two ideas now lead you to wonder whether women's purses could be used to advertise businesses (it works for T-shirts, why not for purses?). The point here is not to judge prematurely whether an idea works or not, but to let the creative ideas bubble and surface of their own accord.

A psychologist by the name of Sarnoff Mednick developed a theory of creativity that focused on the concept of remote associations—that is, creativity could sometimes be seen as the result of two rather different ideas coming together in a new and unusual combination. For example, we don't ordinarily associate ice cream with cooking, but a number of desserts, like Baked Alaska, depend exactly on this combination. Mednick developed a test called the "Remote Associates Test" to try and assess this ability of combining remote associations. The test consists of triads of words, and the respondent needs to come up with a fourth word that is associated to all three. Consider, for example, the words "uncle," "Dane," and "white shark;" what word might be related to all three? One possible answer is "great." We have "great uncles," "great Danes," and "the great white shark." There may be other answers as well. Consider the examples below, and see if you can come up with an answer to each item (a list of answers are given in the appendix, but, again, keep in mind there may be other answers possible).

1.	elephant	tree	baggage
2.	bird	airplane	insect
3.	plumber	rattle	dance
4.	glad	cards	black
5.	surgical	investigation	electric contact
6.	strategy	depart	sign
7.	Olympus	God	Nirvana
8.	teach	hard knocks	marm
9.	wrestling	kick	cut
10.	China	elements	ware
11.	annoyance	balloon	judge
12.	Jerry	drum	Thumb
13.	piece	magazine	keeper
14.	beetle	tree	dog
15.	angel	persistent	Marx
16.	knee	hat	top
17.	nasty	golden	average
18.	cigar	Cuba	Gila
19.	general	file	offensive
20.	evergreen	apple	yearn
21.	foot	mistle	hold
22.	stroke	ceremony	sergeant
23.	heaven	book	chess
24.	ago	distance	house
25.	fat	paint	palm

Oppositional Thinking

Have you ever met people who seem to take pleasure in being "oppositional"? If you point out to them a cute red dress in a store window, they will tell you it's not red, but maroon and, furthermore, it is very ugly. If they are driving, and you ask them to turn right, they will turn left, and if you ask them to go slower, they will speed up. Most people, I think, prefer not to be oppositional and will even keep quiet rather than express a contrary opinion. For most of us, there is little attractive about oppositional thinking, but it can be useful in creative problem-solving. For example, you are on a committee to beautify your neighborhood. Rather than brainstorm all the ideas to make the neighborhood beautiful, try to generate a lot of ideas on making the neighborhood uglier. As paradoxical as this may sound, some of the ideas may in fact, when revised, serve as springboards for some creative solutions for your initial challenge. Part of the reason why oppositional thinking can work is that it is seen as a game, and people who may have difficulty thinking of good positive solutions may be able to enter into the spirit of the game and not be concerned about looking foolish—after all, it is just a game.

Consider one of the following statements:

1. "George W. Bush is one of the best Presidents we've ever had."

2. "The idea of God is a superstitious relic from the past."

3. "Adultery should not be considered a crime or immoral."

4. "The world would be better off if the Nazis had won the Second World War."

5. "The majority of politicians are sincere, honest individuals who contribute greatly to the betterment of their community."

6. "Abortion is a right of every woman."

Most likely you have fairly strong feelings about each statement and can easily take a pro or con position (at least in the privacy of your home). Now, imagine you are a member of a debating society, and you need to argue the *opposite* of what you really believe. For example, you really believe that Bush is an excellent President, but now you need to argue the opposite. What evidence would you marshal? What points would you make?

> The Ferris wheel is a delightful invention (unless you are really afraid of heights) that has charmed and enchanted generations of people. The Ferris wheel, invented by George Washington Gale Ferris, made its debut at the Columbian World Exposition in Chicago in 1893. It was colossal in size, with a diameter of 250 feet and a carrying capacity of 2,160 passengers. The main axle weighed over 45 tons and was, at that time, the largest single piece of steel ever forged. Ferris's idea was met with great skepticism. His idea was labeled a "barbaric contraption," "too fragile," and Ferris was ridiculed as "the man with wheels in his head." But he persisted, and his passion, his enthusiasm, and perseverance brought the project to fruition. The Ferris wheel became the central attraction of the World Exposition.

WISH WITH ALL YOUR MIGHT

Most of us have, at one time or another, wished for something that might have been impossible to achieve. "I wish I were as rich as Donald Trump." Or "I wish I were as physically attractive as George Clooney." Or "I wish I were as tall as..." Or perhaps something more mundane, such as "I wish I didn't have to eat all those Brussels sprouts." Or you might have wished for something quite possible, which at the time seemed out of reach—"I wish that cute guy/gal in my class would notice me."

The "I wish" approach can be an important tool in creative problem solving. For example, in trying to come up with easy to prepare menus for dinner, a parent might wish for "complete meals that could be prepared in 10 minutes," or "low calorie desserts," or "a meal so delicious there would be no leftovers," or "I wish I could get my kids to try some new recipes." Another parent might wish for "food that could be reconstituted simply by adding water," or "cans that do not need a can opener to open." These wishes could serve as springboards to either identifying the "real" problem (not enough time to prepare good meals) or alternate solutions (perhaps everyone in the family should take turns preparing a meal).

Speaking of wishes, did you hear the story of the three religious leaders who were shipwrecked on a desert island? They were a Jewish rabbi, a Protestant minister, and a Catholic priest. They built themselves some shelter and were surviving relatively well with the food on the island. One day, they came across a bottle with the proverbial Genie who granted each a wish. The rabbi said: "I had a family that I miss and a lovely congregation. I wish I were back home." With that, he disappeared in a puff of smoke—his wish was granted. The minister, too, said he had a family that he sorely missed, and he too disappeared in a puff of smoke. The priest thought awhile, and then said to the Genie, "I didn't have a family, so quite frankly there is no one back home that I miss. But I sure miss these two guys, and I wish they were here..."

Exercise Your Imagination

Leff (1984) wrote a charming little book called *Playful Perception*, a guide to experiencing the world in imaginative and creative ways. He suggests a number of interesting exercises including the following:

1. Imagine that everything around you is alive. The pencil on your desk, the shoes you are wearing, the thermostat on your furnace, the telephone, and even the tissue in your pocket are all alive. If you could hear their conversations what might they be saying? What kind of personality does your thermostat have? What is the pencil thinking as you take notes? How does the telephone feel? What hopes and dreams does the tissue have? What kind of questions would you ask your shoes?

2. Imagine that you are a dog and your owner is taking you for a daily walk. What do you see? What do you feel? What goes through your mind? What do you hope for? What do you enjoy? What do you dislike? If you could talk to your owner what would you say? When you meet another dog, what would the conversation be like? What would you say to the fire hydrant? To the mail carrier? To the cute French poodle (or handsome Great Dane) that lives next door?

3. Many years ago, Marcel Duchamp shocked the Parisian art world by hanging a urinal in an art gallery. Perhaps you have visited an art gallery where what seemed an ordinary object was on display.

   Now look at a particular object near you and imagine that the object is on display in an art gallery, and that art critics are raving about it. Can you appreciate the beauty of that object? What kind of statement does it make to you? What was the artist thinking when creating this object?

For example, as I am writing this, I look at a mug that I use as a pencil holder. It is inscribed "Harvard Medical School" and was a gift from a family member. As I *look* at it, it seems made of beautiful porcelain with a very creamy hue. It has two beautiful gold bands and a heraldic emblem with the Latin word "veritas." The light from the window shines on it and makes very interesting patterns. It is really quite lovely and, despite its beauty, conveys an image of strength and permanence. It speaks of generations of men and women studying the human body and disease, of battles won over yellow fever, polio, and other diseases, and of many challenges still ahead. I feel proud of the person who spent a postdoctoral year in such lofty surroundings, and am somewhat embarrassed that I would use such a mug for the lowly purpose of holding pencils. But then I imagine that mug saying: "I am always at the ready to serve you and provide pencils that capture all your ideas."

4. Painters find inspiration in all aspects of the world—not only the beauty of landscapes and the human body, but also the ugliness of war, the darkness of depression, etc. A few painters are closely identified, at least by the lay public, with a specific source of inspiration. For example, Modigliani painted portraits of women with elongated necks, Picasso painted rather fragmented faces, and Salvador Dali is known for his unique paintings of melted watches in bizarre settings.

   Imagine that you are a highly talented painter. You can paint anything you want. Where would you get your inspiration? What kinds of landscapes or people or whatever would you paint? What colors would you use? How large or small would your canvas be? How might you paint a series of paintings having to do with computers? With microwave ovens? With pocket combs? With discarded food containers? With credit cards? With the keys of a piano?

> Francis Ford Coppola is a well-known screenwriter and film director, with movies like *The Godfather* and *Apocalypse Now* to his credit. He is also a successful winery owner in the Napa valley of California. He attributes much of his success to the polio he was stricken with at age nine. He was confined to bed and isolated from other children. As he sat in bed, he allowed his imagination to take flight. He wrote sound tracks for silent cartoons that he played on a projector, and created plays with puppets.

The Shadow Game

"My shadow is tired of following me." What a marvelous image! I wish I knew who said that. Think if you were your shadow and came to life. What would you do? Why are you tired? What kind of conversation would the shadow have with your self? With the sun? With other shadows?

Hopefully, the above topics have opened up your mind a bit more to the playfulness and excitement of creativity. To perhaps apply an overused image, to be creative you need to show the curiosity, exuberance, and imagination of a child. Did you ever notice that, if there were a puddle outside, every self-respecting child would find it and gleefully jump in it, while most adults would avoid it like the plague? To be creative, you need to jump into the puddle of creativity with as much energy and delight as you can muster.

Chapter 4
The Road to Creativity

Getting Started

Although generating ideas sounds like a fairly simple procedure, often the most difficult part is getting started. How often did you tell yourself that you were going to read a particular book, or look into membership at a physical fitness club, or start a particular hobby, and simply never got started? If you have the passion, that inner motivation, that driven quality that often is present in highly creative people, then there usually is no problem (though even highly creative people experience moments of inaction, paralysis, or writer's block). For most of us, however, we need to be prodded. Here is where habit can become useful.

All you need to do is set aside a specific time and place in which you will "create." The time doesn't have to be extensive—even 10 or 15 minutes is worthwhile. The place can be simple—even just a chair and a card table in a quiet corner of your house are sufficient. All you need is to develop the habit that, at a certain time each day (or every other day, or once a week), you will force yourself to sit and create. It's like brushing teeth. Most of us do pretty well after breakfast, simply because it has become routine; it's programmed into our day. We do less well at other meals, unless we make a special effort to incorporate that tooth brushing into our routine. Once you do, not only does it become a habit, but also, if you miss tooth brushing after a meal, you feel as if something is missing.

Sometimes, the enforced period of creativity can be incorporated into some other routine activity. Some people, for example, find that their daily commute to work is a good time to think and create (especially if you don't have to do the driving). Others find that ideas come more easily while shaving, or having lunch at a desk, or mowing the lawn. The problem is that these situations do not provide the lack of distractions, the solitude, the mechanics for making notes, that a chair and a quiet corner provide.

> Isabel Allende, a wonderful novelist, perhaps best known for her book, *The House of the Spirits*, indicated that, for her, "silence and solitude" are important, particularly as she gets older.

How to Capture Ideas

There is a wonderful old movie called "The Graduate" that starred Dustin Hoffman. He plays a young college graduate from a well-to-do family, who is celebrating his graduation but is also at a loss as to his future plans. A neighbor (the father of the girl he loves, as well as the husband of the Mrs. Robinson he later beds) tells him that the secret of life and future success is "plastics." This was at a time when plastics were a major new product and clearly changing many different aspects of our culture.

In the same vein, I would propose that the secret of creativity is "3 x 5 index cards." I usually carry a bunch in my shirt pocket and, whenever an idea strikes, I try to write it down. Years ago, I wrote a college textbook, *Psychological Testing: An Introduction*, and I developed an extensive collection of 3 x 5 cards on questions from students, materials from newspaper articles, scientific references, convention presentations, and so on. When I finally decided to sit down and write the textbook, those 3 x 5 cards proved invaluable.

So I strongly recommend that you carry a bunch of 3 x 5 cards (I guess a Palm Pilot or other electronic gizmo would do just as well) and get into the habit of making notes. Often, ideas come when a person is relaxed or when a person is away from work, riding on a train, or even in the middle of the night. Be prepared to capture ideas by having 3 x 5 cards available (or a notebook, a tape recorder, a Palm Pilot, or whatever is most comfortable for you). Ideas are like butterflies—they may approach you, but won't stay very long. Don't expect to capture an idea in the middle of the night if you have to go down to your den and turn on your computer first.

When I was teaching college classes, most of the time students would be scribbling furiously, trying to keep up with my lectures. Occasionally, though, I would see some students simply sitting there like couch potatoes, not writing anything down. When I questioned them, they would produce some lame excuse ranging from, "I didn't have a pencil" to "I didn't think what you were saying was important," or even "It's all in the book, isn't it?" Typically, these were the students who did not do well on exams, but, more importantly, they were wasting their brains and had never developed their creativity. I asked them if, as I lectured, they didn't have any ideas of their own, anything they could write down, even a list of groceries. The answer was typically a blank stare.

The American Society of Mechanical Engineers gave Paul MacCready the honorary title of "Engineer of the Century." He is probably best known for his Gossamer Condor, a hang glider contraption that was the first successful man-powered aircraft, and the Gossamer Albatross, the first man-powered aircraft to cross the English Channel. He and his company are also responsible for many more inventions. Even in the middle of conversations, he uses a notebook to jot down ideas, and considers daydreaming, especially when he is on vacation, his most productive activity.

Chester F. Carlson is the inventor of xerography, the dry, non-photographic process that duplicates documents—the process at the heart of the copier machine. His parents were poor and suffered from tuberculosis and other illnesses, so they moved often in search of a more healthful climate. Chester developed into a solitary, introverted, and shy child.

He kept a diary and, by the time he was twelve, was working very hard outside of school hours to help the family. Some of his jobs required that he wake at five in the morning. As a teenager, he worked in a local print shop in exchange for a small, unwanted printing press, which he used to publish a couple of issues of a magazine. This experience led him to think about duplicating processes, and he started a little "inventor's notebook," where he would jot down his ideas. He kept this habit up throughout his career.

Brainstorming

Probably the best-known technique designed to stimulate creative ideas is that of brainstorming. This technique was "developed" by Osborn (1953), although it was actually used by Hindu teachers in India for hundreds of years before Osborn made its use popular in business settings. Brainstorming was very popular in the 1950's and 1960's, although it became quite clear that this was not a magic bullet, but simply a very useful technique to generate ideas.

Brainstorming has four simple rules:

1. Quantity of ideas. The goal of brainstorming is to produce as large a number of potentially creative solutions as possible.
2. Deferred judgment. When ideas are generated, no matter how fantastic or impractical, they are not to be judged until later.
3. The wilder the better. The notion here is that it is easier to take wild ideas and later try to change them into workable solutions. The focus is on imagination, on creativity, on novelty, on fantasy, on the unusual.
4. Combination is sought. Participants are encouraged to use other participants' ideas, embellish them, alter them, and give them a twist and a tweak.

To run a brainstorming session for more than one person, you need a leader who explains the four rules and any other aspects (e.g., "We will stop in 20 minutes"). Usually, participants are asked to "free-wheel," rather than take turns, and some kind of record is kept of the ideas generated, preferably on a blackboard or flip chart where everybody can see them. The leader can also be helpful in prodding the flow of ideas, and in reminding participants of the deferred judgment rule. At the end of the brainstorming period, the ideas generated are then evaluated along everyday constraints, such as feasibility, cost, ease of implementation, and so on. Sometimes, a few ideas stand out as reasonable solutions to pursue, and sometimes not. One possible approach is to select the top five (or eight or ten or whatever) ideas and pursue these in detail. Another possibility is to select not only the *top* five ideas, but also the *bottom* five, the ones that seem most bizarre, impractical, far out, and then pursue all ten ideas in detail. Sometimes, what seems at first to be impractical turns out to be the most interesting.

Brainstorming groups can vary from impromptu or loosely organized meetings to fairly well organized procedures. On the more organized side, there is usually a chairperson (leader, facilitator, consultant, etc.). This person has a number of tasks aside from the obvious ones related to calling a meeting, informing the participants, and making sure the time utilized is well spent. One of the tasks is to make sure that the challenge to be solved is specific and manageable. Challenges like "How do we make this a better world" are simply not useful. Once the problem is stated simply and specifically, the chairperson prepares a memo that states the problem and gives a couple of examples of the type of ideas that the brainstorming group will generate. Members are then selected and provided with a copy of the memo ahead of the actual session. The chairperson should also have ready a list of possible solutions to be used if the actual group session needs to be primed. Another task of the chairperson is to stimulate the flow of ideas by asking questions such as these:

How can we change _____ (e.g., the size, the color, the taste, the shape, etc.)?

Can we substitute _____ (e.g., the color, the type of material, the persons to be involved, the location, etc.)?

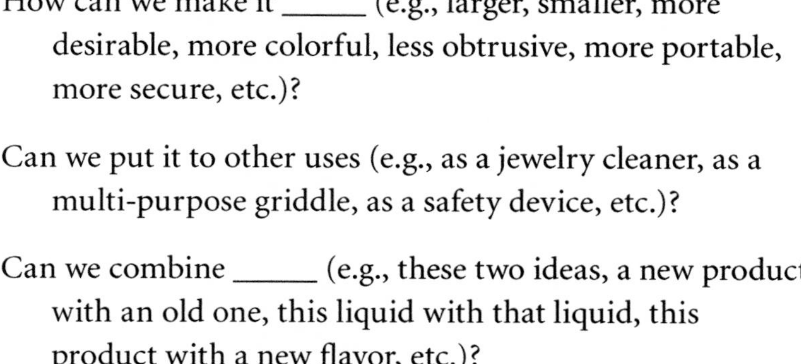

How can we make it _____ (e.g., larger, smaller, more desirable, more colorful, less obtrusive, more portable, more secure, etc.)?

Can we put it to other uses (e.g., as a jewelry cleaner, as a multi-purpose griddle, as a safety device, etc.)?

Can we combine _____ (e.g., these two ideas, a new product with an old one, this liquid with that liquid, this product with a new flavor, etc.)?

Another task of the chairperson is to appoint someone to record the ideas generated. This can be done by one or two people, and may be recorded by type or video recorder. However, the listing of ideas generated needs to be visible to all group members, since "piggybacking" on another person's contributions is an integral part of the brainstorming process. Usually, ideas are numbered so that one can keep track of how many ideas have been generated. The tracking can also serve as a motivational carrot, with the chairperson, for example, suggesting to the group, "Let's get fifteen more ideas."

A well run brainstorming session can generate a lot of ideas, so most sessions don't last very long—somewhere between 15 and 45 minutes seems to be typical. Sometimes, the tempo of the session is regulated by having periods of idea generation followed by periods of quiet time for "incubation" (for example, 3 minutes of idea generation followed by 5 minutes of incubation).

The chairperson follows through after the formal meeting ends and collects any supplemental ideas. This can be done informally by contacting each of the participants on the following day, after each person has had a chance to "sleep on it." Or it can be done in a more formal way by preparing and circulating a list of all the ideas generated at the brainstorming session. Another possibility is just to list the more promising ideas.

Finally, the results of the brainstorming need to be evaluated. Is each idea feasible, cost-effective, in keeping with the company's goals and procedures, etc? Sometimes, the same individuals who participated in the brainstorming session will be the ones to evaluate the ideas, but often it will be a different group.

Over the years, all sorts of variations of the brainstorming procedure have been developed. In one, each participant independently writes down one or more ideas. The papers are then passed to the next person, who may write a modification of the idea or a new idea. The papers are once again passed, and the procedure continues until everyone has had a chance to look at and possibly contribute to all the ideas. Other variations intersperse the brainstorming time with periods of evaluation. This serves to focus on what may potentially be the most useful ideas. If the potential group of participants is very large, like a college class or attendees at a conference, the larger group can be broken down into smaller groups, and then the larger group can be reconvened and the results from smaller groups shared.

Improving, Not Inventing

One of the key ideas of brainstorming is that it is quite all right to "piggyback" on someone else's ideas. You don't need to invent; improving can be quite lovely. So, in that framework, how would you improve:

Toilet paper?

The daily newspaper?

Men's shoes?

Zoological gardens?

An art museum?

An ice cream cone?

Some Brainstorming Problems

Here are some challenges for brainstorming practice:

How can I increase my income?

How can aggressive driving be reduced?

How can paper towels be made to last longer?

How can we better welcome newcomers to our community?

How can we reduce the use of military force to solve conflicts?

How can we raise funds for the local school?

How can we promote healthier eating in our families?

Although many people may not quite recognize the name, Ben Cohen is the Ben of Ben and Jerry's ice cream. He has been described as an "incredibly creative visionary entrepreneur." Certainly, the fact that Ben and Jerry started with an ice cream parlor in Burlington, Vermont and within fifteen years transformed that parlor into a publicly held company with annual sales of more than $100 million speaks for itself.

Brainstorming: A Final Word

Research psychologists, being what they are, have attempted to research all sorts of questions related to brainstorming. These include:

What's the most effective group size? A size of ten to twelve persons seems good.

Should participants know ahead of time what the focus will be? On technical or complicated problems, it might be best to have the participants informed of the focus a couple of days in advance, so they can go through a preparatory stage.

Should the participants be homogeneous in their technical training and background? For example, would we want a brainstorming group of twelve chemical engineers, all of whom are water-recycling experts? Probably not; a heterogeneous group seems more effective. Obviously, extremes need to be avoided. It might not be productive to have, as one of the participants, the CEO of the company, or to include a child with a group of adults.

Should the original group evaluate the feasibility of the ideas generated? Maybe yes and maybe no…maybe a different group…

Is brainstorming always successful? No, it is only a technique that may or may not work.

Can the group be a one-person group? Yes, in fact, individual brainstorming can be very useful, particularly if the person keeps in mind the idea of deferred judgment.

Use Checklists

One way to jump-start the creative process is to use checklists, and a good beginning is to use checklists that are readily available, such as dictionaries, phone books, and catalogues. If, for example, you are a business person looking for new target customers for a new product, you might want to browse the yellow pages of the phone book to identify various occupational groups. Let's say you've invented a pair of shoes for people who must stand a lot; who might your potential customers be? A perusal of the yellow pages might suggest store clerks, waiters, chefs, mail carriers, dance instructors, house painters, and so on.

We have all used this approach when we are looking for a gift for a specific person. We browse in stores; we look at catalogues and check advertisements to find that perfect gift. The problem here is that we are creatures of habit. We go into the grocery store and, despite the valiant efforts to have us buy new products, we tend to buy the same things, week after week. The next time you're in the grocery store, look at the items purchased by other customers in line. Chances are you'll see a number of items you have never considered buying, and perhaps don't even know where they are located in the grocery store.

In the area of creativity, one of the most basic and useful "checklists" was presented by Osborn (1953), one of the pioneers in the area of creativity as applied to the world of work. Here are some of his checklist items:

How could this product be modified for a new use?

To what other uses could this be put?

What other ideas does this suggest?

How can we modify this product?

How could this be changed for the better?

Can we make it bigger? Smaller?

What can be added to make it stronger?

What ingredient can be added to make it taste better?

How can this be streamlined?

Can the order be changed?

I suggested to my college students that they spend 15 minutes a week browsing in the library in sections that were not directly relevant to their chosen field. For example, if they were Psychology majors, I would urge them to look at the Oriental studies section, or books on Engineering, or the medical school journals. If they came across something interesting, I would urge them to make notes on 3 x 5 cards. Often, students reported back that these little excursions had opened their minds to other fields, and that they were able to use some of the ideas they had come across in term papers and other endeavors. One enterprising young man even used the line, "I just read a fascinating article in the American Medical Journal" to impress young ladies at the local bar.

Attribute Listing

Another technique to creatively solve problems is that of attribute listing, which is made up of two parts: attribute modifying and attribute transferring (R. P. Crawford, 1978). Let's say that our problem to be solved creatively is to come up with new ways to sell toothpaste. Most toothpaste comes in a tube, so we would list the attributes of that product: color, type of package, flavor, smell, consistency, and so on. These attributes could be further broken down; for example, color could be color of the toothpaste, color of the tube, color of writing on the tube, color on the outer package. Under each of these attributes, we could then generate possible ideas. For example, under color, we might list different colors (purple, azure), combinations (striped, polka dots), colorless, or even changing colors (white that becomes green when the user has brushed sufficiently).

Writers have been known to generate plots for books, screenplays, and so on by identifying major attributes, such as heroine, setting, major conflict, motivation, secondary plot, etc., then listing under each of these a variety of possibilities. For example, under heroine we could list orphan, abused spouse, CEO of a company, mad chemist, medical resident, young lawyer, archaeologist, etc. Under setting, we could list a Jewish neighborhood in Brooklyn, emergency room in a hospital, the outskirts of Mogadishu, Somalia, etc. From each attribute we might randomly pick a specific component and put these into what might be a very creative book outline—the adventures of a female medical resident in a small town in Somalia during the 1890's who has a strong phobia about horses but loves to play poker, and is looking for a Jewish rabbi who cheated her at poker during a visit to Brooklyn!

A variation of this approach involves taking two attributes at a time and listing these in a spreadsheet fashion. For example, for our toothpaste challenge we might take color and flavor and list them thus:

	COLOR			
FLAVOR	White	Green	Black	Purple
Mint				
Cherry				
Honey				
Cheese				
Cinnamon				
Spinach				

We can then evaluate the combinations: White mint? Black mint? White cinnamon? Purple spinach? Still another variation is that, once we've listed some attributes, we could then take one attribute and list objects or activities that share that attribute. For example, with our toothpaste challenge, we might list the attribute of "minty." Now, what else is minty? We might think of crème-de-menthe liqueur, Life Savers candy, chewing gum, Vicks VapoRub, mint jelly, tabouleh, the US Mint, money, etc. Now, would any of these jog our creative thinking? Could we, for example, include a collector's coin with each tube of toothpaste? Could we put a coupon worth $1000 in a few tubes of toothpaste (or on the inside of the tube, so the toothpaste has to be used before the customer can determine whether they won)? Could we develop a chewing gum that also cleans teeth? Or toothpaste that would be rubbed on the teeth rather than brushed?

All of the above has to do with the first part: attribute modifying. The second part is attribute transferring, which is really analogical thinking. To get back to our example of toothpaste, we could ask, "What else is like toothpaste?" Would thinking about chalk, mustard in a squeeze bottle, the lead in a mechanical pencil, hair spray, etc. help generate ideas? Other questions that can be asked are:

What can we copy (cans of shaving foam)?

What works well with other products (caulk comes in tubes and is applied with a caulking gun)?

Where could we find ideas (could we look at chewing gum flavors for ideas)?

Erle Stanley Gardner was a practicing attorney who became a prolific writer best known for the eighty-two Perry Mason mysteries that he authored. He was a very hard-working person who set himself a quota of 1,200,000 words a year. This was in the days before computers, and for many years he typed his manuscripts with only two fingers. In fact, he was so prolific that many believed he had a staff of writers to assist him. The president of his publishing company offered the sum of $100,000 to anyone who could prove that Gardner had not written all of his own material. Such proof was never found.

Gardner realized that each of his mysteries was made up of components. He listed these (e.g., characters, situations, complications, etc.) on a "plot wheel" with various spokes. He would spin the wheel, and the spokes would align in different combinations. Each combination would provide him with the outline of his next book. His first Perry Mason book was published in 1933. In that same year, Gardner also published sixty-nine novelettes or short stories, and his second Perry Mason book. Between 1895 and 1965 there were 151 mystery books that sold over a million copies—of those, ninety-one had been written by Gardner. (Hughes, 1978)

THE SPREADSHEET APPROACH

We can expand the attribute listing approach by what I call the spreadsheet approach. The first step is to identify the major dimensions of our problem. Again, let us use the challenge of selling more toothpaste. We might identify, as our major dimensions, the following: purpose of toothpaste, size of container, and pricing options (this is easier to diagram if not more than three dimensions are listed). Now, for each dimension, let us list three or four subheadings. For example, for toothpaste we might list: prevent cavities, clean teeth, refresh breath, and clean jewelry. For size of container, we might list: small, medium, and large. For pricing options, we might list: economical, average, and expensive. Now we can diagram these as follows (see Fig. 1):

We now have 36 (4 x 3 x 3) possibilities to consider. For example, we might consider creating a toothpaste product that refreshes breath, is medium in size, and expensive in price. It might be marketed in a velvet pouch rather than a cardboard box, have a fancy name, and be advertised solely in magazines whose readership consists of financially successful readers (*Architectural Digest*? *Wine Spectator*?). Or we might consider a product with all four purposes, but small in size and economical in price. Perhaps this product could come in small tubes, with a dozen tubes packaged in a can and sold in grocery stores.

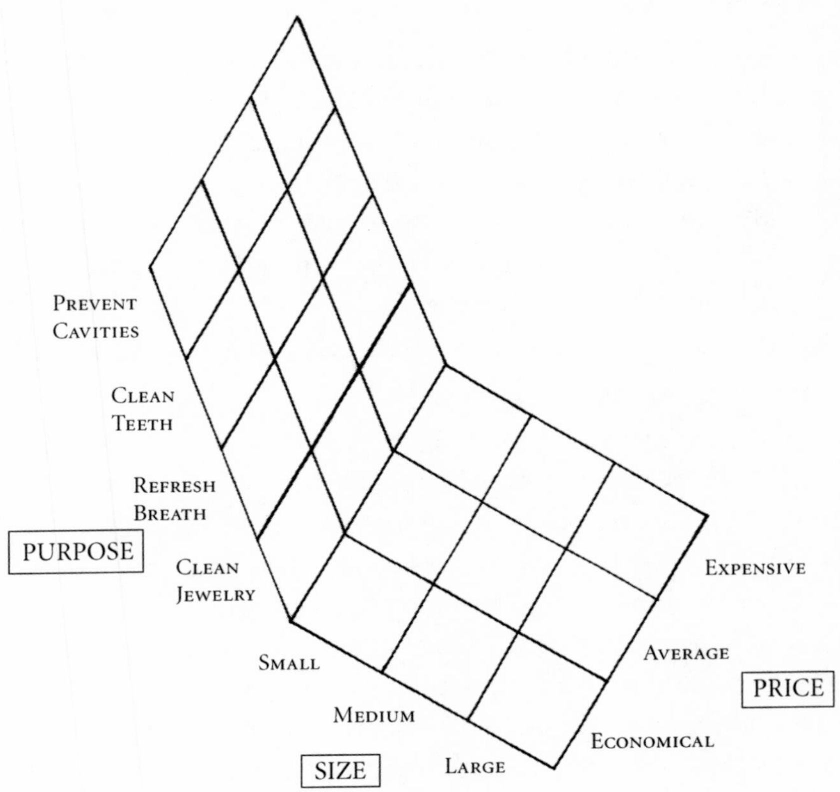

FIGURE 1

This approach can also be analyzed using templates other than a cube. For example:

TOOTHPASTE

PURPOSE	SIZE	PRICE	CONSISTENCY	FLAVOR
Prevent cavities	Small	Economical	Paste	None
Clean teeth	Medium	Average	Semi-liquid	Mint
Refresh breath	Large	Expensive	Liquid	Cherry
Clean jewelry			Gas	Rum

We can now run through our table and select one from each column to see whether the resulting combination might jog our thinking. For example, could we create toothpaste that prevents cavities, in a medium container, that is expensive, in a liquid form, with the flavor of rum?

Forced Relationships

Another technique that can be used to produce creative solutions is that of "forced relationships," where two items that are ordinarily not related are considered together. For example, think of a chair and a ball. We can now think of a chair on four little balls (casters)—i.e., the typical office chair. But why four? Why not five, or six, or two hundred? We can also think of a chair where the seat and the back are made of two inflatable balls to provide a firmer or softer cushion for the user. Or perhaps chairs for sports enthusiasts with a sports symbol emblazoned on the back—a golf ball, a football, a basketball, etc. from a specific team or player. Or perhaps a chair with a tennis ball embedded in its back to force good posture. What about a chair not made of wood or metal, but of the materials that golf balls are made of? Or a floating chair made of cork like the inner core of a baseball? Some chairs fold; is there a way to make a ball fold for easy storage? You can sit on a chair; how about sitting on a ball (have you ever seen a bean bag)? If you go to a gym or a physical therapist, you might have seen rather large balls that are used for a variety of exercises. What about an exercise chair, one that could serve the dual functions of sitting and exercising?

> Richard Drew was an engineer who went to work for the famous 3M company in St. Paul, Minnesota. At that time (1923), 3M made sandpaper. Drew was testing a particular type of sandpaper at a local automobile body

shop when he noticed that the mechanics were having a difficult time making clean dividing lines on two-color automobile paint jobs. As a solution, Drew developed the first masking tape. Subsequently, he was testing this masking tape to determine how much adhesiveness it should have. One of the mechanics told Drew to take the tape back to his "Scotch" bosses and have more adhesive put on it. The name stuck…and Scotch tape was born….

Be a Tourist at Home

Most of us have taken on the role of tourist a number of times. We arrive in a city or location that is new to us, and we notice the architecture, the people, the parks, and the shops. We are surprised (sometimes, not pleasantly) at the high prices of souvenirs, but we discover the perfect gift to send to Aunt Veronica back home. We compare the tourist setting with our own neighborhood and perceive similarities, as well as differences.

Now, imagine you are a tourist in your own neighborhood. Take a walk or bus ride as a real tourist might. Do the people you meet seem somewhat different? In what ways? Go into a store that perhaps you have never, or rarely, entered and look at the items as a tourist might. Are there objects that might capture the essence of your part of the world? How do you think someone from Somalia or England might perceive your local stores, the streets, the grass lawns, the houses and apartment buildings?

Note that you are being given two rather separate challenges. One is to take on a role, that of a tourist. Taking on a specific role often changes perception—think, for example, how a bus driver sees the route differently from a passenger. So one good way to change perception is to alter your everyday role. Secondly, you are being asked to take on the role of someone else—in this case, a tourist from Somalia. Facility in taking on the role of another person is often a hallmark of creativity. Perhaps this is why works of art can move us profoundly—because the artist has captured some emotion or event that we have experienced in our own life. Taking on the role of another can facilitate both creative thinking and evaluative thinking. By taking on the role of another (for example, a potential customer), we might be able to come up with creative solutions that our own everyday role would not permit us. Taking on the role of another (for example, the boss) might also allow us to evaluate whether our creative solution will be embraced or not (and, perhaps, ways that we might sell that solution to our skeptical boss).

Be a Camera

If you have more than a passing acquaintance with a camera, you realize that lighting and shadows can create major differences in the outcome. Perhaps you have seen photographs by Ansel Adams or other professional photographers, and were amazed at how marvelously clouds and mountains and trees looked because of the shadows and placement of light.

In this exercise, you are asked to take a few seconds from your busy schedule and pretend you are a camera (or a professional photographer). Look, really look, at the scene before you. Whether it's a pastoral scene with grass and trees, or a busy urban street with lots of traffic, focus on the light, on the shadows, on how the sun reflects differently on different surfaces.

Be an Obituary

The older I get, the more morbidly fascinating I find the obituary columns in the newspaper. As the well-known writer, John Grisham, said, "I love the obituaries." I look at the local newspaper to see if any of my fellow university faculty members have died (particularly, the few I disliked immensely…), and I find the write-ups quite fascinating, from the initial disclaimer (the person didn't die, but "was embraced in the arms of the Lord" or "was reunited in heaven with her husband," "her head peacefully stopped the rhythm of life," or the person "peacefully crossed over") to the narration of the person's accomplishments ("his collection of miniature pigs won third prize at the county fair"). Quite often, I wish I had known the person while they were still alive, and am enchanted by the love and admiration expressed by the survivors.

Imagine that you are given the opportunity to write your own obituary. What would you say? What really describes you as an individual? How have you influenced those who know and love you? What contributions, if any, have you made to your community? What skeletons in the closet would you definitely not want to reveal?

If you find this exercise too depressing, select someone else, like a political figure that is still alive, and write the obituary for that person. The intent here is to use your imagination to do a task that requires imagination.

John Grisham is probably one of the most successful novelists, especially if success is measured by number of books sold or placement in bestseller lists. Grisham grew up in Mississippi; his father was a construction worker, and the family was quite poor.

As a writer, Grisham shows the value of having a schedule: he starts a book in August and finishes by November. His latest book, *The Innocent Man*, is the story of Ron Williamson, a baseball player in the minor leagues from Oklahoma, who was arrested and convicted for the rape and murder of a woman. He was sent to death row for twelve years and was eventually exonerated by DNA evidence. His mental problems became very serious, and he was labeled insane. He eventually died at age fifty-one of cirrhosis of the liver. Grisham happened to read Williamson's obituary and was galvanized by it.

Be a Newspaper Reporter

My understanding is that newspaper reporters are trained to ask the following questions: Why? Where? When? Who? and What? So, in reporting a crime, they want to report why the victim was killed, where the crime occurred, when it took place, what will happen, and what is the importance of this crime. We can also add the question how—how was the crime committed?

These same questions can also be very useful in trying to solve a creative challenge. Suppose, for example, your boss asks you to come up with some ideas to make better use of the suggestion box by the employees' water fountain. You might ask yourself: Why did the boss ask me? Is this task better done by others? Why is it necessary? Is the boss not getting any suggestions? Is the company running quite smoothly? If not, why are employees not making suggestions?

Where should the suggestion box be placed? Are there better ways to make suggestions than through a box? When should suggestions be made? Should there be a form enclosed with one's weekly paycheck? Should there be a specific time designated as "suggestion time"? Who should make suggestions? Should the suggestions be anonymous? What happens to the suggestions? Do the employees know what happens? Should the suggestions be posted? Should they be rewarded? What concerns and questions does the boss have?

How should the suggestions be handled? If a new procedure is developed, how will it be promulgated? How will it affect employees?

I am sure that, with some reflection and "incubation," you can come up with more and better questions. But keep in mind the task of a reporter; it can be a useful framework.

Put Off Till Tomorrow

In our highly organized and hectic life, we tend to want to solve problems immediately. Don't know what to have for dinner? Stop at the grocery store or deli and get take-out. The air conditioning unit is not working? Call the repairman. Similarly, when faced with a problem requiring a creative solution, we tend to want closure, to consider and implement a solution as soon as possible. But the process of creativity has its own ebb and flow and cannot be rushed. In fact, it is best to allow the creative juices to percolate, to simmer, and to sleep on it. Let your mind do the work—don't push it into premature closure.

Redesign the Human Body

One of the more fun exercises I used with my students in classes of creativity is the following:

> One day St. Peter approached God and, feeling particularly brave, said, "You know, God, when you created Adam and Eve, you really didn't do such a hot job. The human body could really stand some improvements."
>
> God smiled with amusement and said, "Okay, Pete, what improvements would you suggest?"
>
> And Peter said, "____________________________."

(Here the students were instructed to fill in the blanks by giving specific, concrete answers and to think of original, but plausible, suggestions.)

Creative Writing

Many of us went through a period in life (usually our preteen or teen years) in which we kept a diary. It's too bad that, as we matured, we typically dropped that activity. Daily writing is an excellent way to increase our verbal skills, enhance our appreciation of the everyday world, communicate with others, and come to grips with our own creativity. Writing a diary has, of course, been replaced by blogging, but the problem with blogging is that personal creativity may be sacrificed due to the public nature of the activity.

At any rate, here is an activity that can be helpful with enhancing creativity, whether you use a yellow pad or a computer. Think of an unusual beginning sentence, and then write one or two pages based on that sentence. Here are some sentences to get you started:

The fastest chicken in the world…
She was walking along the street and suddenly…
What was in that bottle?
The day Uncle Ernie got killed…
Samantha was a cat…
How could I have been so stupid?
Slowly, the door opened and …
Why was my name in the newspaper?
There was the evidence right before my eyes.
The note from my doctor was terse.
I still remember when I first saw her.
The bottle of sleeping pills was …
Please don't hurt me, I said.
It's the year 2076 and…
What a wonderful world this would be if…
I knew it was a scam but…
Why was the street painted purple?
The weirdest dream of all…
Ciao Bella.
My hands were frozen.
I had never seen such big…

"Alupi neri samuni," she repeated.

How could I be in Hong Kong when my flight…

I never knew I had a twin.

Twenty-five years had elapsed but…

What was I thinking!

How could this be happening to me?

I had never seen a real ransom note…

We will come back for you in two months…

The discovery that gold could be extracted from sand…

Slowly, I was becoming blind…

Word Fluency

Fluency, or the ability to generate many responses, is important in creativity, since the more responses you can generate, the more likely it is that you will generate some potentially creative solutions. The more ideas you can generate, the better, even if the majority of those ideas turn out to be duds. Let's suppose, for a moment, that only one idea out of a thousand turns out to be a creative idea. If you generate 3,000 ideas, you very likely will have three creative ideas. But if you generate only fifty ideas, the probability that those fifty ideas will include a creative idea is rather small.

Here are some exercises to increase your fluency:

1. Write down all the words you can think of that have the letter "o" in second place (as in "down", "words", and "you" in the above sentence).
2. Write down all the words you can think of that have the letter "b" in third place.
3. Write down all the words you can think of that begin with the letter "m".
4. Write down all the words you can think of that contain the letter "w", but not in first place.

5. Write down all the words you can think of that contain both the letters "p" and "t" in any order.
6. Write the names of animals that contain the letter "o" (as in "dog").
7. Using all or some of the letters in the word "articulate," write down as many words as you can think of (for example, late, tiara, lear).

WORDS AS BUILDING BLOCKS

Here is a list of words:

impressive	horse	eyeball	demijohn
none	table	stoop	chard
restless	surrey	orange	arrow
façade	robin	nutcracker	public
cruet	pugilist	newscast	crocodile

Try writing sentences that use as many of these words in one sentence (aside from the obvious solution of "The teacher handed each child a list of 20 words…"). Start with a sentence that uses two of these words, then a sentence with three of these words, and so on.

Rearrangement of Words

For each set of words below, rearrange them into a meaningful sentence.

For example: tidy desk not is my
Becomes: My desk is not tidy.

trip to I city recent my the Verona visit of on was able

are to the quite flights long Nepal because wait there two is only

would I recognize longer no afraid was Jim me that

experienced new not was waiter the at restaurant the very

rolled the under pencil newspaper blue had the

but amazing I a them frustrating computers bit really are find quite

MULTI-MEANINGS

Many words have more than one meaning. For example, the word ball refers not only to a round object such as the kind of ball used in baseball, but it also means a fancy dance, as well as having fun (I'm having a ball). Write down all the words you can think of that have more than one meaning.

WORDS WITHIN WORDS

Try to think of words that contain other words within them. For example, the word "example" contains the word "ample," the word "nonelectrical" contains "non," "one," "elect," and "electrical," and the word "arpeggio" contains "peg."

NEW WORDS

New words are continually entering our vocabulary, especially words associated with computers, such as blog, e-mail, google, and Ipod. There are also new words in other areas, such as bling, carjacking, and baggravation (a blend of the words, bag and aggravation, and referring to the feeling experienced by air travelers when their baggage doesn't show up). What if you were in charge of inventing new words? What would they be, and what would they mean? For example, I would propose "onel" as meaning a new coffee drink with one shot of latte, and "repud" as someone who left the Republican Party. What would you propose?

Eat Your Words

Did you ever consider the fact that much of our language relates to food, even when we are not speaking about food? Consider, for example, that an attractive woman is described as a "peach," a "tomato," or even a "chick." We describe someone as "full of beans," or showing the "milk of human kindness," or tall as a "bean pole." What other food expressions can you think of?

Incomplete Figures

In the late 1960's, a psychologist named Paul McReynolds developed a test called the "Obscure Figures" test as a measure of innovation. The subject was presented with forty doodles, asked to indicate what each doodle might represent, and to do so in an imaginative way. Here is a doodle. What might it be?

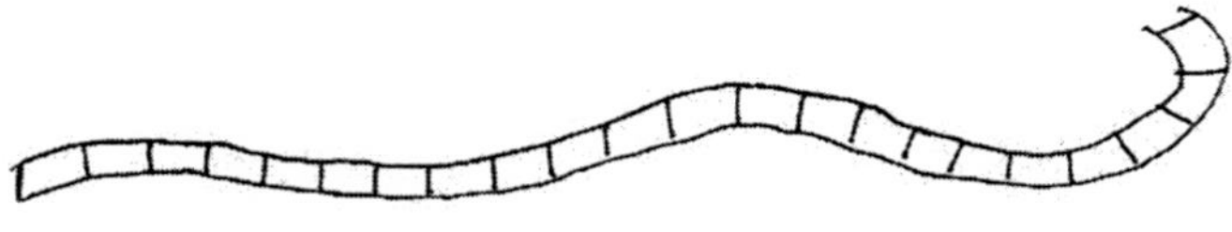

Figure 2

One person might respond by saying "railroad tracks," but a somewhat more innovative response might be "a caterpillar," "part of the intestinal tract," "a twisted piano keyboard," "a sugar cane growing horizontally," or even "twenty-three boxes of paper clips following a mild earthquake."

Here are some other doodles (see Fig. 3). What might each represent? Give as many responses as you can. Try to be innovative, but your responses should be "understandable" to another person—i.e., they should fit the doodle.

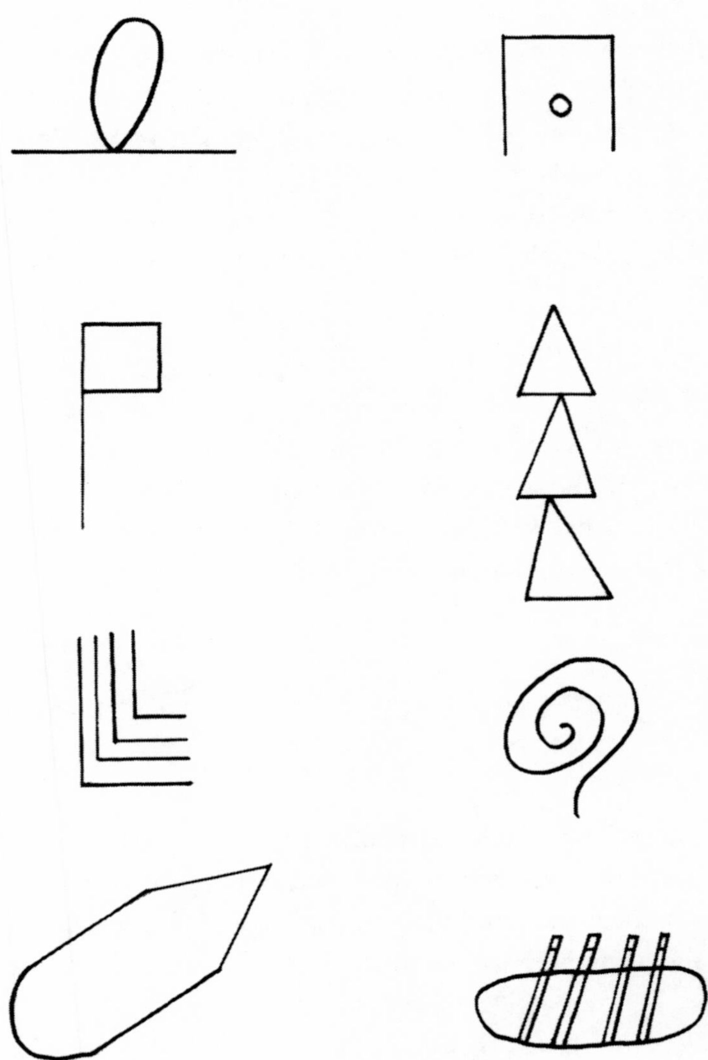

FIGURE 3

AND MORE INCOMPLETE FIGURES

Complete these figures any way you like (see Fig. 4). Make believe you will be submitting the results to a teacher, who will grade them for novelty and creativity (but not drawing competence).

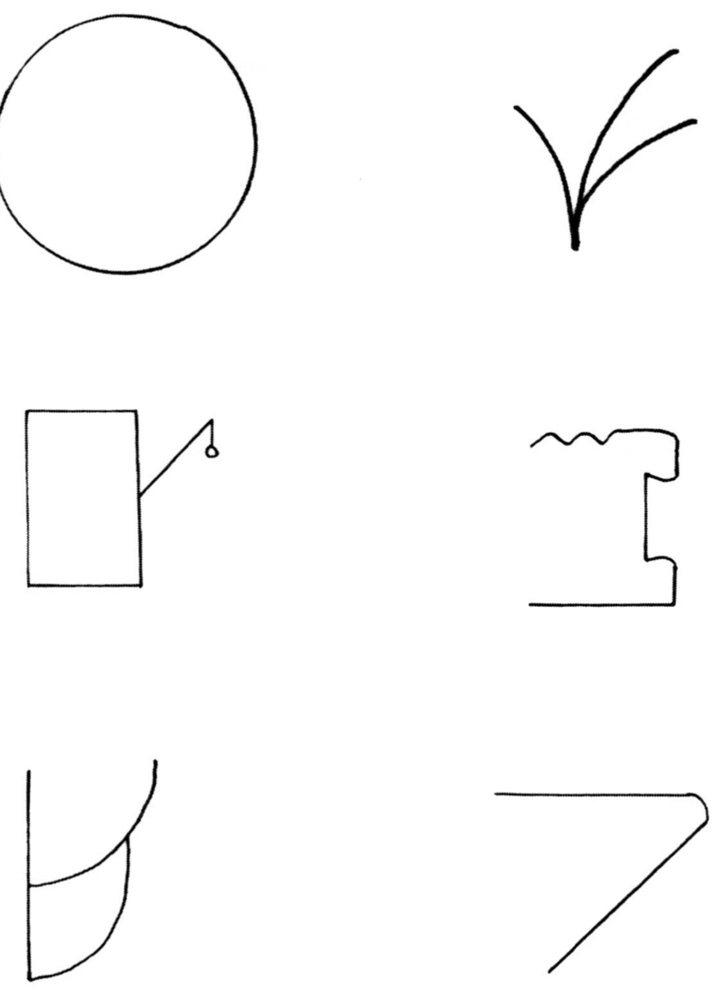

Figure 4

WHAT ELSE?

Consider a simple object like a kitchen knife. It is used to cut and slice. But what else could it be used for? You could use it to open letters, to clean your fingernails, as a fishing spear when attached to a bamboo pole, to play "spin the bottle" if you didn't have a bottle, as a weight at the end of a rope if you wanted to sling the rope over a tree limb, as a screwdriver, as a yardstick (my son is 8 and 1/2 knives tall…), as a marker between two properties, and so on. Some uses may be more practical than others, but the emphasis here is on novelty (try this exercise the next time you have friends over for dinner!)

For each of the objects below, consider how many different ways that object might be used, in addition to its basic uses. As in the example above, try to withhold critical judgment!

Coffee mug

A box full of paper clips

An Ipod that no longer works

One half of a pair of pliers

A card table

A screwdriver

A recent issue of *Time* magazine

What's My Line?

Many years ago, in the infancy days of television, there was a very entertaining show where a panel of distinguished personalities tried to guess the occupations of various guests by asking true-false questions. This exercise also involves guessing occupations, but instead of convergent thinking (what is *the* occupation of this person), we will use divergent thinking.

Certain symbols are associated with specific occupations. For example, the caduceus (a staff with two entwined snakes and two wings at the top) is a symbol for physicians, while a retort (a glass container with a long beak) is a symbol for chemists. Along these lines, we might consider a pencil as a symbol for writers, reporters, pencil manufacturers, accountants, or even motivational speakers who urge us to get the lead out!

What occupations might be symbolized by the following?

a stone	a dog	clouds	a violin
a shoe	a rose	a book	a howdah[1]
a sewing needle	a computer	an airplane	a shrimp
a rabbit	a tooth	a piccolo[2]	a stela[3]

Now let's approach it from the other side. Take the occupation of electrician. What symbol might we assign to it? One answer might be a light bulb; another might be a thunderbolt. If you've used an electrician recently, you might be tempted to symbolize that profession with a dollar sign or a Lexus automobile! Perhaps a light switch might come to mind, or an electrical meter, or even an electric chair! Or perhaps the letter "E" embellished in some way, or the formula from physics that shows the relationship between watts, amps, and volts. The possibilities are many.

Now consider what symbols might come to mind for each of the following occupations:

garage mechanic	bartender	airplane pilot
firefighter	stockbroker	beekeeper
high school teacher	janitor	dentist
barber	lion tamer	fasion model
lawyer	minister	realtor
bricklayer	dance instructor	soccer player
physician	oculist	marine biologist
clown	perfume manufacturer	poet
private detective	garbage collector	dog groomer

BECOME ANOTHER PERSON

Since we are talking about occupations, imagine that you could choose to be anyone and anything that you wanted to

1 The seat on an elephant or a camel

2 A small flute

3 A carved stone slab

be. If, for example, you could trade places with anyone, whom would you select? Your next-door neighbor? The President of the United States? A movie star? Why?

You probably have heard the story about the three nuns who die and arrive at the Pearly Gates. There, they are met by St. Peter, who tells them they have lived such good lives of sacrifice and giving that they now have six months more to live as anyone they choose. The first nun replies that she would love to be Sophia Loren and gets her wish. The second nun selects Marilyn Monroe, and she too disappears in a puff of smoke. The third nun tells St. Peter that she wants to be "Sara Pippelini." St. Peter is at a loss and tells the nun he does not recognize that name. The nun hands him a newspaper. St. Peter reads the headline, starts laughing, and tells the nun that the headline says, "Sahara Pipeline laid by 1200 men in six months."

Imagine you are one of those nuns (or a priest). If you were given another six months to live as someone else, who would that person be? Also imagine your *least* preference.

What If?

One of the key questions to ask when trying to solve a challenge creatively is to ask "What if…?" For example, what if we made this product smaller? Or what if we added some color? Or what if we gave it away for free?

Imagine that, overnight, the human body became like that of an amoeba—that is, if we lost an arm in an accident, we could easily grow a new one. The same for a hand, or finger, or any body part, for that matter. How would the world change? Here is what one person said:

1. Most surgeons would become unemployed.
2. Hospitals would take their operating rooms and surgical wards and turn them into lounges.

3. Soldiers would become fiercer in hand-to-hand combat.
4. Sausage would no longer be an acceptable food, as sausage makers would become quite careless.
5. Teenagers would experiment cutting off various body parts.
6. The wheelchair industry would go broke.
7. Health insurance policies would be cheaper.
8. The word "crutches" would be dropped from the vocabulary.
9. The topic of conversation at cocktail parties would no longer be "Is this your second marriage?" but instead "Are those your original legs?"
10. Scientists would blame global warming for this event.
11. The saying, "He charged me an arm and a leg," would take on new meaning.
12. Politicians would tax any new appendages.

Now you try to imagine the consequences of each of the following:

1. What if, all over the world, daily temperatures only fluctuated between 55 and 75 degrees Fahrenheit?
2. What if each household had to get their own drinking water, and the only source were clouds?
3. What if tubes of toothpaste were only sold in a 2-pound size?
4. What if everyone became a strict vegetarian?
5. What if no one committed any crimes?
6. What if cars could be powered by carrot juice?
7. What if shaking hands became illegal?

8. What if all adult human beings were equal in height, say 6 feet, and weight, say 180 pounds?
9. What if, overnight, the entire populations of the United States were transported to Russia, and the Russian population to the United States?
10. Imagine that you have invented a razor blade that maintains its sharpness as it gets used.
11. What if you had eyes in the back of your head?
12. What if toothpaste were declared a health hazard?
13. What if the police department no longer monitored automobile traffic?
14. What if trees came in different colors, like purple, red, and chartreuse?
15. What if we had to pay greater taxes the more garbage we produced?
16. What if alcoholic drinks were no longer intoxicating?

Imagination at Work

Imagine you are driving to work or to the grocery store. If you don't drive, imagine you are on a bus going to work or the grocery store. Go over the route mentally and try to picture in your mind the stop signs, highway exit signs, and other guideposts you usually pass. Now, go over the same route mentally, but instead of the usual stop sign imagine that the sign has a message for you. What might that message be? For example, here are some messages on a client's imagined stop signs:

You are late for work.

Your hair looks particularly nice today.

Beware of men wearing polka dot pants.

Stop eating peaches.

Eat simnel (this is a nonsense word).

Creosote or bust.

If you have a creative challenge, imagine that the signs will provide you with some potential answers. What do the signs say now?

Imagine you are somebody's pet—a dog or a cat. What would your name be? What would the name reflect about the kind of dog or cat you might be? What if you were called Muffin? Or Baby? Or Stupid? Or Killer? What four or five aspects about being a dog (or a cat) would you like the most? The least? What would your owner be like? What would your neighborhood be like? Are there any experiences you might have as a dog or cat, but not as a human being?

> One of the most imaginative, creative writers was Jules Verne, who wrote fantastic adventures that took place underneath the sea, in hot air balloons, and all around the world. His *Around the World in Eighty Days* is still a marvelous classic. But Jules rarely left his home, nor did he travel to any of the fantastic places he wrote about—except in his imagination!

HUMOR CAN BE LIBERATING

Humor is one of the elements of creativity. By humor, I don't necessarily mean jokes or the kind of sophomoric humor found in a lot of cartoons and comic strips. Here I am referring more to the appreciation of the human condition that often can be quite humorous—the kind of humor found in Neil Simon's plays or Gary Larson's "Far Side" cartoons. Creative individuals are often characterized by a sense of humor, a playfulness through which they approach life. Note that many jokes and puns involve "playing" with the meaning of words or grammatical rules.

Here is a simple exercise to activate your funny bone: Your local community college is developing a set of general interest non-credit classes for the community. Below are some tentative possibilities in the guise of potential course titles. Can you suggest others?

1. Career opportunities in Iran.
2. Skate yourself to regularity.
3. Tweeze your way to better hygiene.
4. Tax shelters for the homeless.
5. Obedience training for armadillos.
6. Do-it-yourself liposuction.

> Two friends, Jim and Bill, are out in the woods hunting. Suddenly, Jim keels over and appears to be dead. In fact, Bill can't feel Jim's pulse. In a panic, he dials 911 on his cell phone and reports that his friend has just died, and he doesn't know what to do. The well-trained emergency operator tells him to keep calm, and that the first thing is to make sure that Jim is really dead. There is a brief pause in the telephone conversation, and then the emergency operator hears a gunshot. Then Bill gets back on the cell phone and says, "Okay, what do I do next?"

More Than Cognition

Most of us are cognitive individuals—that is, we are guided by our cognitions: our thinking, our knowledge, our logic and rationality. We are guided by our brain (it is said that some men aren't, but that's another story…). In most of this book, I have discussed creativity as if it were primarily cerebral, a part of intelligence, of cognition. It is also much more.

To be creative means to be sensual—that is, to use all of our senses. So, in facing a creative challenge, don't forget your senses.

Approach a problem from the viewpoint of smell—could we create a new toothpaste that simply smells fresh? Or that smells like lavender or musk? What about touch? Could we design a cardboard box that would be fun to touch? Or, conversely, that children would not touch? If we were thinking about redecorating our room, how would we do it emphasizing touch? What if we were blind?

Movement

So far, most of the exercises in this book have to do with imagination, with words. There is, however, a dimension of creativity that has to do with kinesthesia—the sense that is mediated by your body's movements. I am sure you have admired dancers—whether ballet, mambo, waltz, or some other type—who move so gracefully and can interpret musical themes through their almost liquid body movements. You can see this same sense in top athletes, and in a few people who seem to be at one with their bodies. For many of us, our body is not what we wish, and we feel awkward when we try dancing, roller-skating, or other physical activities. Here, then, is an exercise that you can do in the privacy of your room:

Try to imagine what it would be like to move like a giraffe—and then do it!

How about moving like:

A lazy dog

A lion chasing a deer

An ant foraging for food

A fig tree growing branches

A piece of paper swaying in the breeze

A Venus flytrap

A mummy that is still alive

Use Your Fingertips

Because we are mostly verbal and visual animals, we don't ordinarily use our other senses. But, in many ways, creativity requires our full involvement. So here is a fingertip exercise:

Using your fingertips, "caress" the top of your desk, a granite counter, sand at the beach, the bark of a tree, and the surface of your car. As you do this, concentrate on the bodily sensations you are receiving. Imagine that you have never seen a granite counter. What does it feel like? Is it cold? Smooth? Does it tickle your fingers? Is caressing granite a pleasant sensation?

Make believe that you are blind. Run your fingers over your face. Run your fingers over a friend's face. Does the sensory input match what you know about yourself and about your friend? Is it a pleasant sensation? Do different parts of the face have different textures? Suppose you were to select a spouse based only on how their face felt to your fingertips; what would you "look" for?

Sensory Awareness

Most of us scurry through our world like hungry rats in a maze. We pay attention to those things we have to—the sale sign at the store, the stock market report, and the partly hidden motorcycle cop—but rarely do we "stop to smell the flowers." One way to enhance creativity, to become more fully aware, to stretch our senses, is to make "sensory awareness" a daily habit. For a start, at least once a day stop and pay attention to your senses. Here are some suggestions:

1. Do stop and smell the flowers, whether it's a plant in your own garden, in a florist shop, a grocery store, a public garden, or wherever. You don't have to be a master gardener to smell a flower, to note the symmetry of the leaves, the color of the petals, to hear the buzzing of the bees, or feel the velvety texture of the stem.

2. Watch the sky for a few minutes. Sunrise and sunset are particularly beautiful, even if you live in an urban area. Look at the color of the sky, the texture of the clouds, the changing interplay of light and shadows.

3. Smell the aromas of food preparation. Look at the water boiling for a pot of pasta. Really look at the color and shape and texture of green beans. Imagine those green beans the size of a pumpkin or the shape of an apple.

4. Focus on a pattern for 20-25 seconds. It might be the shirt you are wearing, the back of a lounge chair, the light grid on the ceiling, or the façade of a building. Notice whether the lines that form the pattern are straight or curved, what colors are in it, what the material is. Is the pattern pleasant or unpleasant? Does it look hard or soft? What other objects might that pattern be? For example, the pattern on a shirt could also be on the front of a book, a country's flag, a sign to warn motorists, a shower curtain, etc.

5. The next time you see a tree, take a good look at it. Notice how tall it is. How thick is the trunk? Is the trunk smooth? Is there bark on it? How many branches are there? What color are the leaves? What shape? Are there any bugs—ants, caterpillars, etc.—on it? Are any of the roots exposed? Is there any damage to the tree?

YOUR HOUSE

You are probably quite familiar with your dwelling, whether you live in a single family home, an apartment, a condo, a college dormitory room, or someplace else. In your mind's eye, try to imagine what your dwelling looks like. Make believe your head is really a camera, and your brain records on film what you can see in your mind's eye. Now try to imagine what your dwelling looks like from the perspective of:

A pilot in a helicopter
A seagull flying overhead
A mouse in the attic
A cockroach hiding in the kitchen
A fly
A neighbor's dog
Your cat
Your winter coat hanging in the closet
A 2x4 in the wall
The car in the garage

Creative Explanations

Sometimes, people are very good at giving what might be called "creative" explanations. I live in Tucson, Arizona, near the border with Mexico. One year, National Guard members from another state were assigned to this area to patrol the border and call in the Border Patrol whenever illegal immigrants were sighted. These members of the National Guard were bivouacked at various hotels, including a luxury resort. When the story broke in the local newspaper, the National Guard commander was quoted as saying that the reason his men were staying at a very expensive resort was that guests at luxury resorts enjoy seeing men in military uniforms.

At any rate, consider the following scenarios and for each one try to come up with some creative explanations:

1. When you arrive home from work this evening, you find that the outside of your house has been painted a different color. Why?
2. When you go to your favorite grocery store, you find that all the employees are wearing tutus. Why?

3. When the library opened on Monday morning, the librarians discovered that all the books had disappeared, but there was no sign of a break-in. What are some possible explanations?

4. On the news, there is a report of a man who died peacefully in his sleep, yet the police suspect foul play. Why?

TRAFFIC SIGNS

If you drive, you are familiar with most traffic signs. You know that a red, eight-sided sign means stop. A red triangle means yield. A diamond-shaped sign is usually a warning sign of some kind, such as "slippery road" or "steep hill ahead" or the possible presence of animals, as in "animal crossing." A sign that is pennant-shaped tells where passing is or is not allowed.

Imagine that a new set of signs is to be developed to inform motorists of each of the situations below. What might each sign look like?

1. There is a motorcycle cop ahead with a radar gun.
2. The next two restaurants have consistently been described as "worst food within one hundred miles of here."
3. The scenic view up ahead really is worth stopping for.
4. The motorist is about to enter an area where other motorists are typically quite rude.
5. For the next five miles, cases of road rage are quite common.
6. At intersections, you must yield the right of way only to vehicles driven by the elderly.
7. The next 5 blocks contain a high concentration of high-school-age drivers.

8. Drivers with arms out of the window are not giving hand signals, but are drying their fingernails.
9. There is a very nice “package” or liquor store in two miles, with plenty of cold beer.
10. There is a “house of ill repute” two miles from here.
11. For the next 20 miles, there is no posted speed limit.

Chapter 5
Summary

I began this book with the statement that "creativity is fun; it can be challenging and personally fulfilling." Hopefully, you, too, have found creativity to be so. Creativity *is* fun. In my classes, I have watched serious college students become like little giggling children as they attempted to redesign the human body or come up with new words.

But creativity is also challenging. To grow creatively requires passion and the practice of imagination; to be creative requires tolerance of ambiguity and the willingness to take risks.

In Chapter 1, I attempted to share with you some basics about the nature and nurture of creativity, without becoming too pedantic or professorial. Perhaps a key summarizing idea of that chapter is that "You're not going to get tomatoes if you haven't planted tomatoes." If you are going to study creativity in a scientific manner, as many psychologists have, it is important to have a precise definition of creativity that will guide your theoretical framework and empirical research. But if you are interested in simply having a good, basic understanding of what creativity is, then the ideas I covered in Chapter 1 are quite sufficient.

Trying to understand creativity is like looking under the hood of a car. If you don't know much about automobile engines, you will only see a very discouraging jumble of wires, widgets, and tubes. On the other hand, if you realize that an engine is made up of a number of components or systems, you no longer perceive that engine as a single mysterious entity, but as a number of parts that, under optimal conditions, work smoothly together. In some ways, this is the message of Chapter 2. To understand creativity, one must perceive the components, the building blocks of creativity. I focused on a couple of dozen such components. There is nothing magical about that number; some components can be collapsed into one, and other components could be further subdivided. But, certainly, such components as curiosity, passion, imagination, metaphorical thinking, and tolerance for ambiguity are crucial to the enterprise of creativity.

In Chapter 3, I focused on a few broad topics that are basic to the development and enhancement of creativity. Central to creativity are dreams, or perhaps more correctly "dream reports." Whether dreams are reflections of our inner unconscious motivation or simply represent a biochemical "exfoliation" is, for our purposes, irrelevant. Considerable evidence exists to support the theory that dreams can be helpful in solving problems, particularly those problems that require visual thinking.

Another major concept related to creativity is the notion of association, the idea that creative solutions often reflect two or more disparate ideas that ordinarily do not occur together. The trick is to force such ideas to come together, to associate, and Chapter 3 discusses several approaches that accomplish this.

Finally, in Chapter 4 I listed a number of specific procedures designed to enhance creativity. Some of these, like brainstorming, have been studied intensively, while others have not. Where possible, I gave authorship credit, but most of these exercises can be found in multiple sources with no clear authorship. Still others are original and were developed in my creativity laboratory for teaching or research purposes.

I believe that all of the procedures discussed in Chapter 4 can be quite helpful in developing creativity. Finally, keep in mind that being creative is very much like being fit. You can't diet for one week and do strength training for two weeks and expect to be fit for the rest of your life. Being fit involves a lifestyle that is continuous, designed to keep your weight under control and your good health at a premium. So with creativity! Reading this book is a good first step, but you must continue to fuel your passion, to exercise associative thinking, to increase your curiosity, to play with words, to brainstorm, and to spend time looking at the world in imaginative ways. The good news is that these activities are fun and, when practiced frequently, they can become second nature.

Additional Readings & References

Cohen, G. D. (2000). *The Creative Age.* New York: Avon Books.

Crawford, R. P. (1978). "The Techniques of Creative Thinking," G. A. Davis & J. A. Scott (Eds.), *Training Creative Thinking.* Melbourne, Fl.: Krieger.

Davis, G. A. (1992). *Creativity is Forever* (3d ed.). Dubuque, Iowa: Kendall/Hunt Publishing Co.

Edwards, O. (2006). *Smithsonian*, October, pages 32-35.

Gardner, H. (1993). *Creating Minds.* New York: Basic Books.

Gordon, W. J. J. (1961). *Synectics.* New York: Harper & Row.

Heppenheimer, T. A. (1989). "King Lear," *Invention & Technology*, Spring/Summer, Vol. 5, #1, pages 34-45.

Hughes, D. B. (1978). *Erle Stanley Gardner: The Case of the Real Perry Mason.* New York: William Morrow & Co.

Kher, U. (2006). Creatology. *Time*, October, page A34.

Mansfield, H. (1992). "The Razor King," *Invention and Technology*, Spring, Vol. 7, No. 4, pages 40-46.

Miller, R. H. (2006). *Stan Lee: Creator of Spider-Man.* Detroit, MI: Thomson-Gale.

Orlean, S. (2007). "The Origami Lab," *The New Yorker*, February 19 & 26, pages 112-120.

Osborn, A. F. (1953). *Applied Imagination.* New York: Scribners.

Parnes, S. J. (1981). *Magic of Your Mind.* Buffalo, NY: Bearly Limited.

Prince, G. M. (1970). *The Practice of Creativity.* New York: Harper & Row.

VonOech, R. (1983). *A Whack on the Side of the Head.* New York: Warner Communications.

Solutions

Answers to remote associations (page 87):

1. trunk
2. wing
3. snake
4. hand
5. probe
6. exit
7. heaven
8. school
9. scissors
10. table
11. trial
12. Tom
13. Time
14. bark
15. harp
16. cap
17. mean
18. Havana
19. rank
20. pine
21. toe
22. master
23. match
24. long
25. grease

Answers to rearrangement of words (pages 119-120):

On my recent trip I was able to visit the city of Verona.

Because there are only two flights to Nepal, the wait is quite long.

I was afraid that Jim would no longer recognize me.

The waiter at the new restaurant was not very experienced.

The blue pencil had rolled under the newspaper.

Computers are really amazing, but I find them quite a bit frustrating.

Printed in the United States
137877LV00001B/1/P

9 781935 437017